DSM-5™
Essentials

10668415

DSM-5™ Essentials

The Savvy Clinician's Guide to the Changes in Criteria

LOURIE W. REICHENBERG

WILEY

Cover image and design: David Riedy

This book is printed on acid-free paper. ♾

Copyright © 2014 by John Wiley & Sons, Inc. All rights reserved.

Published by John Wiley & Sons, Inc., Hoboken, New Jersey.
Published simultaneously in Canada.

For general information about our other products and services, please contact our Customer Care
Department within the United States at (800) 762-2974, outside the United States at (317) 572-3993
or fax (317) 572-4002.

Wiley publishes in a variety of print and electronic formats and by print-on-demand. Some material
included with standard print versions of this book may not be included in e-books or in print-on-
demand. If this book refers to media such as a CD or DVD that is not included in the version you
purchased, you may download this material at http://booksupport.wiley.com. For more information
about Wiley products, visit www.wiley.com.

ISBN: 978-1-118-84608-7 (paper)
ISBN: 978-1-118-84609-4 (ebk)
ISBN: 978-1-118-84613-1 (ebk)

Printed in the United States of America

10 9 8 7 6 5 4 3

CONTENTS

PREFACE

In writing this book on *DSM-5 Essentials*, I set out to serve three purposes:

1. To inform readers about the changes from *DSM-IV* to *DSM-5* in an organized and concise manner so they could carry on the important work they do with clients, students, and colleagues without undue disruption.
2. To provide background material, criteria, and limited treatment recommendations for new disorders that are making their debut in *DSM-5*.
3. To provide, whenever possible, a list of *ICD-9-CM* (clinical modification) and *ICD-10-CM* codes with the intention of simplifying the billing process and providing a handy all-in-one tool.

This book, then, serves as a supplement to *DSM-5* and *ICD-9* and *ICD-10*.

Introductory material provides the history of the *International Classification of Disorders*. It is included because the *DSM* and the *ICD* are classification systems that continue to merge and change at their own pace over time. I found it important to understand the distinctions between them, their strengths and weaknesses, and why we need both. Some readers may choose to skip that part and go directly to Chapter 1 and a discussion of the *DSM-5* disorders. Similarly, many readers will not be interested in coding. They can easily skip over the lists of codes at the beginning of each category.

As the coauthor of *Selecting Effective Treatment: A Comprehensive Systematic Guide to Treating Mental Disorders, with DSM-5 Update*, now in its fourth edition, my long-term interest is in advancing the best evidence-based treatments for specific diagnoses. Although that is not the focus of this book, I hope that readers will tolerate any slips on my part into discussion of treatment modalities, especially as it applies to the new *DSM-5* diagnoses. Readers who are interested will find a wealth of such information in the aforementioned book.

I would like to acknowledge Dr. Gary Gintner, University of Mississippi and past president of the American Mental Health Counselors Association, for his generous and helpful recommendations. He read a version of this text and provided detailed suggestions for its revision.

I would also like to acknowledge the other reviewers of this manuscript, who provided concrete suggestions for improvement.

Finally, I would like to give a warm and special note of gratitude to Rachel Livsey, senior editor, and to the staff at John Wiley & Sons, who have ushered this book through the production process. Rachel has been an enthusiastic, helpful, and responsive companion on this incredibly short journey, and I am 100% certain that this book would not have been possible without her involvement.

I would also like to acknowledge the following reviewers for their thoughtful comments and feedback: Shana Averbach, LMFT, private practice and RAMS, Inc., San Francisco, CA; Jay Noricks, PhD, private practice, Las Vegas, NV; Jodi Bassett, LCSW, High Focus Centers, Paramus, NJ; Lori Puterbaugh, PhD, LMHC, LMFT, NCC, Troy University; St. Petersburg College, Seminole, FL; Pat Giordano, LPC, NCC, ACS, Director of Home-Based Services at Bridges, Member-at-Large for the Connecticut Counseling Association, Adjunct Professor at Southern Connecticut State University, Hamden, CT; Carol Kerr, PhD, Licensed Psychologist, Chief Psychologist, APA-accredited Pre-Doctoral Psychology Internship, Graduate Clinical Training Program, Marin County Health and Human Services, Division of Mental Health and Substance Use Services, Greenbrae, CA; John Arden, PhD, Kaiser Permanente, Petaluma, CA; Faith Drew, PhD, LMFT, CEAP, marriage and family therapist, Charlotte, NC; and Naomi Angoff Chedd, MA, LMHC, BCBA, child and family therapist in private practice, Lexington and Brookline, MA.

HOW TO USE THIS BOOK

R eaders have told us they want a quick and easy way to get up-to-speed on the recent changes to the two main classification systems they use for diagnosis and coding of mental health disorders:

1. The *Diagnostic and Statistical Manual of Mental Disorders*, 5th edition (DSM-5), published by the American Psychiatric Association
2. The *International Classification of Diseases* (ICD), published by the World Health Organization

The publication of the fifth edition of the *Diagnostic and Statistical Manual of Mental Disorders* (DSM-5) by the American Psychiatric Association in May 2013 changed the diagnostic criteria for many disorders, created some new disorders (e.g., hoarding, binge eating disorder, skin excoriation), and removed a few disorders from the *DSM*. It is not surprising if clinicians are confused! The goal of this book is to highlight these changes, no matter how small, in a logical and systematic manner so that readers can easily make the transition from *DSM-IV* to the new *DSM-5*.

For each diagnosis, the reader will be alerted to any changes from *DSM-IV* to *DSM-5*, given information on the implications of these changes for diagnosis and assessment, and advised as to how these changes may affect treatment. When additional information is necessary for further clarification, the specific pages in *DSM-5* are provided so that readers can find the exact information needed to make an accurate diagnosis.

For busy professionals, or their office staff, who need coding information as well, both the *ICD-9-CM* and the *ICD-10-CM* codes are included in this book. At the beginning of each classification category is a handy list of disorders discussed in that section. Each disorder is preceded by the *ICD-9-CM* code and followed by the new *ICD-10-CM* code. When necessary, additional coding information (course specifiers, etc.) is made available in the form of a Coding Note.

The goal was to provide a concise, easy-to-read supplement to give health-care providers, college professors, clinicians in practice settings, and office staff who do coding for insurance reimbursement the information they need to do their jobs smoothly and efficiently. We have not included a lot of jargon, nor a lot of history about disorders. There simply is not enough space to include everything in a publication of this size. However, a thorough explanation is provided of the two different classification systems we have come to rely on for the diagnosis of mental disorders in the United States—the DSM-5 and the *International Classification of Diseases*. As a practicing clinician and former adjunct professor of abnormal psychology, I know what information I needed to be able to continue doing my job.

Many people have suggested that this is Cliff Notes for clinicians, and I have to disagree. This book should be viewed as a supplement to DSM-5 and the ICD-9 and ICD-10, not as an alternative to them. It is my hope that this book provides the information readers need to seamlessly continue their daily work, until such time as they need more in-depth information. This book also presupposes that readers are familiar with the DSM-IV and DSM-IV-TR. Therefore, when a DSM-IV diagnosis was not changed in DSM-5, that is noted, but limited discussion is added.

In writing this book, I followed the new classification structure of DSM-5. The former DSM-IV organization of chapters was based upon clinical or expert consensus, while DSM-5 draws upon data regarding how disorders actually cluster together. The disorders flow in the same direction as DSM-5 and whenever possible I have tried to include lists and an organizational structure that follows a logical, systematic outline and includes callouts in the text, when I thought it would be helpful.

I have not included an explanation of the reasons behind every DSM-5 change, a discussion of both sides of all controversial issues, or a philosophical discussion justifying (or not) the existence of the DSM-5. Those discussions are beyond the scope of this book.

It is also possible that experts in a particular diagnostic category will know more about one specific disorder or another. In such cases (e.g., autism spectrum disorders, adult ADHD), what is included here provides the essence or the backbone of the DSM-5 criteria for the disorder. As new journal articles are published and professional organizations develop new practice guidelines, time will fill in the blanks. Readers are also reminded that the DSM-5 is an evolving document, and that with the assistance of technology and the Internet, regular updates, corrections, and changes are available online.

Clearly, it is not possible to include everything of note in a book of this length. Even so, I believe I have touched on the bulk of the changes in

DSM-5. After reading this book, I hope professionals will feel comfortable in their knowledge and armed with the information they need to conduct diagnoses based on *DSM-5*. In cases in which the diagnostic criteria or coding information may be complicated or confusing, I have tried to be transparent in identifying the resources and the page numbers for further investigation. Above all, I hope that this book benefits clients and ensures that they receive the care they deserve.

Chapter 1

INTRODUCTION

In May 2013, the fifth edition of the American Psychiatric Association's *Diagnostic and Statistical Manual of Mental Disorders* was published. The *DSM*, along with the *International Classification of Diseases* (*ICD*), are the two classification systems that mental health professionals turn to for the assessment, diagnosis, and coding of mental disorders. Both classification systems are important for clinicians, because the code numbers that the *DSM* uses are those listed for similar disorders in the *ICD*. Both sets of codes (*ICD-9* and *ICD-10*, which takes effect in 2014) are included in *DSM-5* and in this book. Following a discussion of the major changes to *DSM-5*, a brief history and explanation of how to use the World Health Organization's *ICD* codes will be provided.

INTRODUCTION TO *DSM-5*

Over the past 60 years, the *Diagnostic and Statistical Manual of Mental Disorders* (*DSM*), published by the American Psychiatric Association (APA), has become the standard reference for mental health professionals in the United States. With the publication of the fifth edition earlier this year, *DSM-5* (APA, 2013a) has become more consistent with WHO's *International Classification of Diseases Clinical Modifications* (ICD-CM, the coding system used in the United States).

DSM-5 incorporates years of research about the brain, human behavior, and genetics. Thousands of experts participated in more than 160 task forces, work groups, and study groups over a 12-year period to research, measure, and conduct field trials of diagnostic criteria for the mental health disorders. In December 2012, the Board of Trustees of the APA approved the final changes that now constitute *DSM-5*.

All of the additions or substantive changes to *DSM-5* were supported by research and planned with the intent to improve diagnosis and treatment, and

1

to be able to be incorporated into routine clinical practice. According to the APA, all changes were "intended to more clearly and accurately define the criteria for that mental disorder. Doing so helps to ensure that the diagnosis is accurate as well as consistent from one clinician to another—benefiting patients and the care they receive" (APA, 2013b).

These and other enhancements to DSM-5, such as changes in the organizational structure, use of dimensional and cross-cutting measures, and consistency with ICD codes were planned to increase the manual's clinical utility and enhance its value for clinicians and researchers alike.

To help clinicians conceptualize and diagnose disorders, DSM-5 is divided into three sections:

> Section I provides a basic introduction on how to use the new manual, how to diagnose using a nonaxial system, and a new definition of a *mental disorder* as a syndrome that causes clinically significant problems with cognitions, emotion regulation, or behavior that results in dysfunctional mental functioning and is "associated with significant distress or disability in social, occupational, or other important activities" (APA, 2013a, p. 20).
>
> Section II provides 20 classifications of disorders that focus on diagnostic criteria and codes.
>
> Section III, Emerging Measures and Models, includes assessment measures, cultural formulation, an alternative model for personality disorders, and conditions for further study.

The Appendix of DSM-5 features highlights of the changes made from DSM-IV to DSM-5, glossaries of terms and cultural concepts of distress, and ICD-9 and ICD-10 codes.

We turn now to a more detailed look at several important changes in DSM-5 that will impact how clinicians conceptualize the diagnosis of mental disorders: the elimination of the multiaxial system of diagnosis, the adoption of a dimensional approach to diagnosis, developmental and lifespan considerations, and the expansion of gender-related and cultural considerations.

Using a Nonaxial System

The multiaxial system in DSM-5 has been replaced with a nonaxial system that combines Axis I, Axis II, and Axis III with all mental and other medical diagnoses listed together. This is consistent with how the WHO's *International Classification of Diseases* records diagnoses—listing as many diagnoses as necessary to provide the clinical picture. The principal diagnosis is the one listed first and reflects either the reason for the visit or the focus of treatment.

For example, a person who makes an appointment for treatment of mild depression related to bipolar disorder and who also meets the criteria for borderline personality disorder would be coded as follows:

296.51 Bipolar I disorder, mild, most recent episode depressed
301.83 Borderline Personality Disorder

This indicates that the focus of treatment will be the bipolar disorder.

In keeping with the established WHO guidelines, other conditions that may be the focus of clinical attention will continue to be listed along with the diagnosis to highlight relevant factors that affect the client's diagnosis, prognosis, or treatment, or if they best represent the client's presenting problem. This list of psychosocial and environmental problems has been expanded in *DSM-5* with additional V codes (from *ICD-9*) and Z codes (from *ICD-10*). If the same person in the previous example discusses exacerbation of his bipolar depression as a result of separation from his wife, the coding would look like this:

296.51 Bipolar I disorder, mild, most recent episode depressed
301.83 Borderline Personality Disorder
V61.03 Disruption of Family by Separation or Divorce

The Global Assessment of Functioning scale (Axis V) has also been eliminated in *DSM-5*. In its place, WHO's Disability Assessment Schedule (WHODAS) is included as a measurement of functioning. This useful tool can be found in *DSM-5*'s Section III. Additional assessment measures are included in the print version of *DSM-5* and online at www.psychiatry.org/dsm5

DSM-5 reassures us that a multiaxial system is not required to diagnose a mental disorder, although that system has been adopted by many insurance companies and governmental agencies. The elimination of the multiaxial system brings *DSM-5* more closely inline with WHO's nonaxial system of diagnosis.

Dimensional Approach to Diagnosis

DSM-IV was based on a categorical system of classifying disorders that assessed the presence or absence of a symptom. This system of categorization had many shortcomings, as many diagnoses are not discrete entities that fit neatly into categories. The result was excessive comorbidity, fuzzy boundaries between disorders, and excessive reliance by clinicians on the NOS (not otherwise specified) category (Jones, 2012).

DSM-5 takes a dimensional approach to diagnosis, providing dimensional and cross-cutting assessments to increase clinical utility and enhance diagnostic specificity on the part of clinicians.

In many instances, separate disorders are not really separate at all but are actually related conditions on a continuum of behavior, with some conditions reflecting mild symptoms, whereas other conditions are much more severe. Consider, for example, bipolar disorders as a spectrum. Individuals can present with a range of symptoms from mild (cyclothymia), to moderate (bipolar II), or more severe (bipolar I). DSM-5 adopts the spectrum concept for many disorders, including substance abuse, autism, and schizophrenia. Using a spectrum approach allows clinicians to consider disorders on a continuum of severity.

In DSM-5, specifiers have also been added to many of the disorders to enhance diagnosis and increase clinical utility. When provided in DSM-5, specifiers apply to the client's current presentation, and only when the full criteria for a disorder have been met. Various types of specifiers in DSM-5 include:

- Course (e.g., in partial remission)
- Severity (e.g., mild, moderate, severe)
- Frequency (e.g., two times per week)
- Duration (e.g., minimum duration of 6 months)
- Descriptive features (e.g., with poor insight)

In DSM-5, a number of cross-cutting measures and assessments are provided to measure symptoms frequently observed in clients regardless of their presenting concern. These assessments can be used in the initial assessment interview to measure other symptoms the client may be experiencing (e.g., anxiety, depression, substance abuse), and readministered at a later date to monitor treatment progress. Two levels of cross-cutting measures are available. Level 1 measures provide a screening tool for the presence of 18 different symptom areas. If symptoms indicate, a Level 2 screening can be conducted. Turn to Chapter 3 for a complete list of assessment tools provided by the APA in the print version of the DSM-5 and online.

Use of Other Specified and Unspecified Disorders

In DSM-5, clinicians are given two alternatives to the catchall "Not Otherwise Specified" category. "Other Specified Disorder" and "Unspecified Disorder" can be used when full criteria have not been met for a disorder, according to the following restrictions:

1. *Other specified disorder.* This category enables the clinician to identify presentations in which the symptoms are clinically significant, but do not meet the full criteria for a disorder, and to state the specific reason why the diagnostic criteria for any given disorder has not been met. For example, other specified bipolar and related disorder can be diagnosed

in the following four distinct ways: (1) persons with a history of a major depressive disorder who now meet all but the duration criterion for hypomania (i.e., at least 4 consecutive days); (2) persons who meet the duration criterion but have too few symptoms of hypomania to meet the overall criteria for bipolar II; (3) the presence of a hypomanic episode without any history of major depressive disorder; and (4) short duration cyclothymia (less than 24 months) in which hypomania and depressive symptoms are present for most days but do not meet the full criteria for MDD, mania, hypomania, or a psychotic disorder. (The duration criterion is reduced to less than 12 months for children and adolescents.) In the presence of this constellation of symptoms, other specified bipolar and related disorder would be the diagnosis.

2. *Unspecified disorder.* If the presentation is clinically significant and does not meet the full criteria for a disorder, and the clinician chooses not to specify the reason that the criteria have not been met (e.g., insufficient information as what might occur in an emergency room setting), the "unspecified" diagnosis would be given. In the example given above, it would be recorded as "unspecified bipolar and related disorder."

These two options are available for all disorders and give clinicians more flexibility in diagnosing cases in which clinically significant distress is noted but the client does not meet the full criteria, or the clinician chooses not to specify the reason the criteria are not met if insufficient information is available. A more in-depth explanation of the *DSM-5* approach to clinical case formulation, including discussion of principal diagnosis, provisional diagnosis, coding and reporting procedures, and the use of other specified and unspecified disorders can be found on pages 19–24 of *DSM-5*.

Assessments, Self-Report Measures, and Interviews

While some measures and scales are included in *DSM-5*, such as a handscored simple version of the World Health Organization Disability Assessment Schedule (WHODAS 2.0), the APA recommends clinicians link in to the eHRS (electronic health records) for more complex assessments of symptoms (APA, 2013a, p. 745). WHODAS 2.0 can be used as an assessment scale, and may also be used at regular intervals to track progress.

Besides the WHODAS 2.0, *DSM-5* includes a number of cross-cutting and assessment tools:

- Assessment and cross-cutting symptom measures by age.
- Online measures to determine symptom severity.

- Clinician-rated dimensions of severity for psychotic symptoms.
- The Early Development and Home Background (EDHB) form is helpful for assessing early development as well as home background experiences (past and current) of a child receiving care. Two versions are provided: one to be completed by the child's parent or guardian, and the other to be completed by the clinician.
- The Cultural Formulation Interview (CFI)—A set of 16 questions that clinicians may use to obtain information during a mental health assessment about the impact of culture on key aspects of an individual's clinical presentation and care.
- The Cultural Formulation Interview—Informant Version collects collateral information on the CFI domains from family members or caregivers.
- An alternative model for diagnosing personality disorders.

These helpful diagnostic tools, including the role of Level 1 and 2 assessment measures, are discussed further in Chapter 3. A comprehensive list of assessments available both online and in the print version of DSM-5 can also be found in Chapter 3. Online assessment measures are available at http://www.psychiatry.org/practice/dsm/dsm5/online-assessment-measures

A Developmental and Lifespan Approach

DSM-5 has adopted a new developmental structure for mental disorders, which reclassifies disorders into 20 sections based on their relatedness to each other and their similarities in characteristics. As a result, disorders first diagnosed in childhood are no longer a separate chapter, having grown up, so to speak, and been dispersed into the larger family of disorders. For example, childhood trauma has been relocated to a new chapter on trauma and related disorders, autism spectrum disorder is now found among the neurodevelopmental disorders, and oppositional defiant disorder (ODD) and conduct disorder form the basis for a new classification of Disruptive, Impulse Control, and Conduct Disorders.

Some familiar disorders have been subsumed into other sections or eliminated completely. Asperger's disorder, for example, has been subsumed into the broader diagnosis of autism spectrum disorders. Adjustment disorder has been reclassified as a trauma- or stressor-related disorder. Meanwhile, some disorders have merely changed names (e.g., conversion disorder is now called functional neurological symptom disorder). These and many other changes are addressed in Chapter 2 of this book.

When possible, the *DSM-5* chapters have been organized in keeping with a developmental focus across the lifespan. Classification ranges from neurodevelopmental disorders (conditions that develop early in life, such as autism) to neurocognitive disorders that develop later in life (e.g., Alzheimer's). The chapters in between commonly manifest in adolescence and young adulthood.

Disorders have also been reclassified into clusters of disorders based on internalizing and externalizing factors. Internalizing disorders are those in which anxiety, depression, and somatic symptoms are prevalent. Externalizing disorders have more disturbances of conduct, impulse control, and substance use.

This developmental and lifespan approach is also seen within chapters. As mentioned earlier, disorders that were first diagnosed in childhood are now incorporated into the overall discussion for anxiety, depressive, bipolar, and trauma-related disorders; schizophrenia; and eating disorders. As part of the lifespan developmental focus of *DSM-5*, each disorder, when appropriate, includes diagnostic criteria and specifiers that relate to childhood manifestations and onset.

Two new disorders included in *DSM-5* provide an important developmental bridge between the early recognition of symptoms in childhood and the diagnosis of a full-blown disorder later in life. Disruptive mood dysregulation disorder (which is discussed later in the section on depressive disorders) focuses on the occurrence between the ages 6 to 17 of extreme emotional dysregulation, without assuming that a diagnosis of more severe magnitude will occur in adulthood. Clinicians should also be aware of attenuated psychosis syndrome (APS), which is included in Section III, Emerging Measures and Models, as APS pertains to subsyndromal symptoms of psychosis that may appear in adolescence or young adulthood and might be a precursor to a full-blown psychotic disorder.

Other disorders currently being studied for further consideration also may have taken root in childhood and adolescence. Internet gaming disorder, non-suicidal self-injury, and suicidal behavior disorder are all associated, to some degree, with onset in adolescence. Clinicians who work with young people will want to refer to Chapter 3 for additional information on these emerging disorders.

More Cultural and Gender Considerations

A welcome enhancement to *DSM-5* is the inclusion of additional gender and cultural considerations, where appropriate throughout the text, when symptoms may be informed by a client's gender, culture, race, ethnicity, religion, or geographic origin. Some of the diagnostic criteria have been made more gender sensitive and culturally sensitive, with variations in presentation provided. For example, social anxiety disorder now incorporates the fear of offending others, which may be manifested in some Asian cultures that emphasize the importance of not harming others. The Appendix to *DSM-5* includes more cultural definitions, examples, and clarifications to help clinicians understand how clients from various cultures may express psychological problems. Readers of *DSM-5* will find a comprehensive cultural formulation interview guide beginning on page 750 of *DSM-5*, which provides clinicians with a practical interview tool they can use to conduct person-centered assessments that ask questions about background in terms of culture, race, ethnicity, religion, or geographic origin. All of the gender-related information and cultural concepts included in *DSM-5* have been written and reviewed with the intent of improving diagnosis and treatment for people of all backgrounds (APA, 2013a).

THE *INTERNATIONAL CLASSIFICATION* *OF DISEASES (ICD)*

Most of the world already uses *ICD-10* to classify diseases and other health problems, to code health records and death certificates, and to capture national morbidity and mortality statistics. The *ICD-10* has been translated into 43 languages and is used by 117 countries.

Within the United States, the *ICD-9-CM* (Clinical Modification) is the current version officially used for coding and billing purposes. This is a modified version of WHO's *ICD* codes created by the U.S. National Center for Health Statistics (NCHS) and the Centers for Medicare and Medicaid Services (CMS). The CM versions provide additional detail and are used specifically for medical coding and reporting in the United States (American Psychological Association, 2012).

On October 1, 2014, all U.S. healthcare providers covered under the Healthcare Insurance Portability and Accountability Act (HIPAA) must begin to use the *ICD-10-CM* diagnosis codes. The *ICD* provides the code numbers but limited diagnostic information. On the other hand, *DSM-5* provides more specific and detailed diagnostic criteria and cross-cutting measures to help the clinician make that diagnostic determination. The complete listing of *ICD* codes is available for use free of charge from the WHO website: www.who.int/classifications/icd/en

A Brief History of the ICD

The *ICD* has been the standard diagnostic tool for more than 150 years. It is used to monitor the incidence and prevalence of diseases and other health problems worldwide. This includes epidemiology, health management, clinical purposes, and analysis of the general health situation of population groups.

The ICD system began in the 1850s with the publication of the *International List of Causes of Death* by the International Statistical Institute. This list, which reported causes of morbidity and mortality, was taken over by the World Health Organization (WHO) in 1948, when the sixth revision was published. In 1977, the *ICD-9* codes were published and are still being used, although the *ICD-10* codes were approved in 1990 and came into use in 1994 (WHO, 2010). Most countries are already using the *ICD-10* coding system; only a few (e.g., the United States, Italy) have yet to switch over. The U.S. Department of Health and Human Services has mandated October 1, 2014 as the deadline for switching over to the *ICD-10-CM* for diagnostic code reporting across all of health care, and the implementation of *ICD-10-PCS* (Procedural Coding System) for inpatient procedural reporting for hospitals and payers. Overall, the number of codes will increase from 17,000 codes currently in *ICD-9* to more than 141,000 codes for different medical diagnoses and procedures with the implementation of *ICD-10*.

Although the primary purpose of the *ICD* is to code and record causes of mortality and morbidity (disease or illness), for the most part, those who are responsible for mental health diagnosis and coding will be interested in only a small section of the four-volume series put out by WHO: *The ICD-10 Classification of Mental and Behavioural Disorders*.

The Use of *ICD-9-CM* and *ICD-10-CM* Codes Throughout This Book

The *ICD-9-CM* codes will continue to be used until October 1, 2014, when the United States switches over to the *ICD-10-CM* codes. The *DSM-5* addresses this interim period by providing two code numbers for each diagnosis, an *ICD-9-CM* number that is in bold and an *ICD-10-CM* number in parentheses, which is to be used after October 1, 2014.

Both coding systems have been provided where possible throughout this publication. At the beginning of each diagnostic category, readers will find a list of diagnoses. Each diagnosis is preceded by the *ICD-9-CM* code and followed by the *ICD-10-CM* code. Specifiers are listed when appropriate (see the following example for Social Anxiety Disorder).

EXAMPLE: *ICD* CODES AND *DSM* SPECIFIERS

ICD-9-CM Code	Diagnosis	ICD-10-CM Code
300.23	Social Anxiety Disorder Specify if performance only	F40.10

Readers should note that code numbers for a disorder may appear in two places. For most disorders the number will appear right next to the name of the disorder. However, for some disorders, the coding tries to capture important subtypes and specifiers. In these instances the code numbers will be listed within the criteria itself, as in the following example.

ICD-9 Code	Disorder	ICD-10 Code
Attention-Deficit/Hyperactivity Disorder (ADHD) **Must specify whether ADHD is:**		
314.01	Combined presentation	F90.2
314.00	Predominantly inattentive presentation	F90.0
314.01	Predominantly hyperactive/ impulsive presentation Specify if in partial remission Specify current level of severity— mild, moderate, severe	F90.1
314.01	Other Specified Attention-Deficit/ Hyperactivity Disorder (ADHD)	F90.8
314.01	Unspecified Attention-Deficit/ Hyperactivity Disorder (ADHD)	F90.9

In other situations, the addition of a specifier may result in a change to the *ICD-10-CM* code.

ICD-9-CM Code	Cannabis-Related Disorder	ICD-10-CM Code
305.20	Mild	F12.10
304.30	Moderate	F12.20
304.30	Severe	F12.20

A Few Facts to Keep in Mind About ICD Codes

Every edition of the *DSM* has supplied *ICD* codes. All of the *DSM-IV* code numbers are *ICD-9* codes. So if you look up PTSD in *DSM-IV*, it will have the same code number as *DSM-5*. *ICD-10-CM* is not just an update to the *ICD-9-CM* codes. *ICD-10-CM* follows a new alphanumeric coding scheme, and therefore the codes cannot be converted. The *ICD-10* reminds us that no classification system is ever perfect, that this and other documents used for diagnosis are always evolving, and that diagnosis requires judgment and clinical experience. Readers may want to check errata sheets for *ICD-10* and code revisions for *DSM-5* at www.DSM5.org. Corrections through October 1, 2013, have been made to this text, so readers should be aware that, in some cases, codes in this book differ from those published in the *DSM-5*.

CONCLUSION

It is beyond the scope of this introduction to include a complete assessment of the evolution of the *Diagnostic and Statistical Manual of Mental Disorders*. Interested readers will find such history in the introductory pages of *DSM-5*. The takeaway message clinicians need to know to conduct a diagnosis using the *DSM-5* classification system is the same guidance they have used in the past: A comprehensive clinical assessment must include a complete biopsychosocial assessment of factors that have contributed to, and that continue to sustain, the mental disorder. The underlying goal is to conduct an accurate diagnosis so that the appropriate evidence-based treatment can begin.

Chapter 2

THE 20 CLASSIFICATIONS OF DISORDERS

For ease of use, this book follows the same classification of disorders as *DSM-5* and, when applicable, notes the name changes in parentheses. When looking for a familiar disorder from *DSM-IV* that may have been reclassified in *DSM-5*, it helps to keep in mind that there is a clear rationale behind the reclassification of some disorders and although the order may seem confusing at first, it reflects data on how disorders are related and tend to cluster together. For example, adjustment disorder has been reclassified as a trauma- and stressor-related disorder in recognition of the fact that exposure to a traumatic or stressful event is an explicit diagnostic criterion for this classification of disorders.

To help conceptualize how *DSM-5* categorizes disorders, the 20 chapter titles are listed as follows:

1. Neurodevelopmental Disorders
2. Schizophrenia Spectrum and Other Psychotic Disorders
3. Bipolar and Related Disorders
4. Depressive Disorders
5. Anxiety Disorders
6. Obsessive-Compulsive and Related Disorders
7. Trauma- and Stressor-Related Disorders
8. Dissociative Disorders
9. Somatic Symptom and Related Disorders
10. Feeding and Eating Disorders
11. Elimination Disorders
12. Sleep-Wake Disorders
13. Sexual Dysfunctions
14. Gender Dysphoria

15. Disruptive, Impulse-Control, and Conduct Disorders
16. Substance-Related and Addictive Disorders
17. Neurocognitive Disorders
18. Personality Disorders
19. Medication-Induced Movement Disorders and Other Adverse Effects of Medication
20. Other Conditions That May Be a Focus of Clinical Attention

We now turn to an in-depth discussion of each classification area, beginning with a list of disorders preceded by the *ICD-9* code for each disorder and followed by the *ICD-10* code. After each list is a discussion of the changes from *DSM-IV* to *DSM-5* and the implications for diagnosis. We focus specifically on what has changed from *DSM-IV*, what this means for diagnosis, and the implications of these changes on the selection of effective, evidence-based treatments.

NEURODEVELOPMENTAL DISORDERS

DSM-5 replaces the chapter on disorders first diagnosed in infancy, childhood, or adolescence with a new chapter, Neurodevelopmental Disorders. These disorders first appear in the early developmental period, generally before a child first starts school. The resulting deficits cause difficulties in personal, social, and academic functioning. Some disorders are discrete (e.g., specific learning disorder), whereas some disorders involve global deficits or delays (e.g., autism spectrum disorders). A few new disorders have been added to the Neurodevelopmental Disorders chapter, and some changes have been made to existing conditions.

ICD CODES AND *DSM* SPECIFIERS

NEURODEVELOPMENTAL DISORDERS

ICD-9-CM Code	Disorder	ICD-10-CM Code
Intellectual Disabilities		
	Intellectual Disability (Intellectual Developmental Disorder) (Must specify level of adaptive functioning. Refer to Table 1, *DSM-5*, pp. 34–36, for definitions of mild, moderate, severe, and profound.)	

(continued)

(continued)

ICD-9-CM Code	Disorder	ICD-10-CM Code
317	Mild	F70
318.0	Moderate	F71
318.1	Severe	F72
318.2	Profound	F73
315.8	Global Developmental Delay	F88
319	Unspecified Intellectual Disability	F79
Communication Disorders		
315.32	Language Disorder	F80.2
315.39	Speech Sound Disorder	F80.0
315.35	Childhood-Onset Fluency Disorder (Stuttering) Note: Adult-onset fluency disorder is coded as 307.0 (ICD-9-CM) or F98.5 (ICD-10-CM).	F80.81
315.39	Social (Pragmatic) Communication Disorder	F80.89
307.9	Unspecified Communication Disorder	F80.9
Autism Spectrum Disorder		
299.00	Autism Spectrum Disorder	F84.0

Coding Notes: Must specify if related to a medical or genetic condition, if environmental, or if comorbid with another mental disorder. Criterion A and Criterion B severity levels must be specified.
With or without intellectual impairment, language impairment, or catatonia must also be specified. (Refer to recording procedures, specifiers, and Table 2: Severity Levels in DSM-5, pp. 50–59.)

Attention-Deficit/Hyperactivity Disorder (ADHD)

Must specify whether ADHD is:

314.01	Combined presentation	F90.2
314.00	Predominantly inattentive presentation	F90.0
314.01	Predominantly hyperactive/impulsive presentation	F90.1

Specify if in partial remission
Specify current level of severity—mild, moderate, severe

ICD-9-CM Code	Disorder	ICD-10-CM Code
314.01	Other Specified Attention-Deficit/ Hyperactivity Disorder (ADHD)	F90.8
314.01	Unspecified Attention-Deficit/ Hyperactivity Disorder (ADHD)	F90.9
Specific Learning Disorder		
Must specify if impairment is in:		
315.00	Reading	F81.0
315.2	Written expression	F81.81
315.1	Mathematics	F81.2
Specify current level of severity—mild, moderate, severe		
Motor Disorders		
315.4	Developmental Coordination Disorder	F82
307.3	Stereotypic Movement Disorder	F98.4
Tic Disorders		
307.23	Tourette's Disorder	F95.2
307.22	Persistent Motor or Vocal Tic Disorder	F95.1
307.21	Provisional Tic Disorder	F95.0
307.20	Other Specified Tic Disorder	F95.8
307.20	Unspecified Tic Disorder	F95.9
Other Neurodevelopmental Disorders		
315.8	Other Neurodevelopmental Disorder	F88
315.9	Unspecified Neurodevelopmental Disorder	F89

The above list encompasses all of the neurodevelopmental disorders in *DSM-5*. Disorders that in the past would also have been first diagnosed in childhood (e.g., elimination disorders, reactive attachment disorder) have been relocated to relevant chapters.

We turn now to a more detailed look at each of the neurodevelopmental disorders.

Intellectual Disability (Intellectual Developmental Disorder), Formerly Mental Retardation

Mental retardation has been renamed Intellectual Development Disorder (IDD) in *DSM-5* to reflect changes in U.S. federal law (Public Law 111-256), which replaced the term *mental retardation* with *intellectual disability*. The criteria for IDD has changed, and people with IDD are no longer categorized solely on the basis of IQ, although IQ must be at least two standard deviations from the mean (70 or less).

IDD is characterized by deficits in cognitive abilities (e.g., problem solving, planning, reasoning, judgment) and adaptive functioning. Diagnostic criteria emphasize the importance of assessing both cognitive abilities and adaptive functioning. The severity level (mild, moderate, severe, or profound) of the intellectual disability is determined by the person's ability to meet developmental and sociocultural standards for independence and social responsibility, not by the IQ score. To help determine a diagnosis, a table listing IDD severity levels (mild, moderate, severe, or profound) across three different domains (conceptual, social, and practical) is included on pages 34–36 of *DSM-5*.

A great deal of comorbidity exists among the neurodevelopmental disorders. For example, children born with neurobehavioral disorder due to prenatal alcohol exposure (ND-PAE; formerly fetal alcohol syndrome) often develop mild intellectual developmental disorders (see Seligman & Reichenberg, 2012, p. 51).

Global developmental delay is diagnosed if the severity level cannot be accurately determined. This diagnosis is restricted to children under the age of 5. If the degree of intellectual disability cannot be determined, unspecified intellectual disability would be the diagnosis.

Communication Disorders

The communication disorders begin in childhood and generally follow a steady course, with possible lifelong functional impairment. In most cases, the functions affected involve speech, language, and social communication. The criteria remain the same for the communication disorders in *DSM-5*, with the exception of language disorder, which combines expressive and mixed-expressive language disorders from *DSM-IV* into one disorder and the addition of social (pragmatic) communication disorder, which is discussed next. Overall, *DSM-5* includes the following communication disorders:

- Language
- Speech sound disorder (formerly phonological disorder)
- Childhood-onset fluency disorder (stuttering)
- Social (pragmatic) communication disorder
- Unspecified communication disorder

Social (pragmatic) communication disorder is a new condition. Children who are diagnosed with this disorder have deficits in the social use of verbal and nonverbal communication, including the following:

- Using communication appropriately for social purposes
- Matching communication to the needs of the situation (e.g., speaking differently in a library than at home)

- Understanding rules for conversing (e.g., using nonverbal signals to regulate interaction)
- Difficulty making inferences, if something is not stated explicitly

If restricted repetitive behaviors, interests, and activities (RRBs) are present, then social communication disorder cannot be diagnosed. Some children who are diagnosed with pervasive developmental disorder—not otherwise specified (PDD-NOS) under *DSM-IV* may now meet the criteria for social communication disorder in *DSM-5*. Also, those who meet only the social communication criteria for ASD, but not the other criteria, may be considered for this disorder.

Autism Spectrum Disorder

With the publication of *DSM-5* comes the integration of four disorders into the broad category of Autism Spectrum Disorder. Autistic disorder, Asperger's disorder, childhood disintegrative disorder, and PDD-NOS have been combined into a single category in recognition of the fact that reliability of distinguishing among these groups had been poor, and there is insufficient research to support maintaining them as separate and distinct disorders. The following new diagnostic criteria are intended to improve reliability and decrease the complexity of diagnosis (e.g., *DSM-5* has 11 different ways to meet the diagnostic criteria, whereas *DSM-IV* reportedly allowed 2,027 diagnostic possibilities).

The new diagnostic criteria for autism spectrum disorder are characterized by the presence of the following:

Deficits in social communication and interaction, in multiple domains, including:
- Deficits in social interactions (e.g., lack of reciprocity in conversation)
- Problems with nonverbal communication skills (e.g., lack of eye contact, body language)
- Difficulty understanding relationships (e.g., creating, maintaining, and understanding nuances in behavior)

Restricted repetitive behaviors, interests, and activities (RRBs), such as:
- Repetitive motor movement (head banging, flapping, or rocking)
- Ritualized behavior (verbal or nonverbal)
- Unusually strong interests in unusual objects or perseveration
- Heightened sensitivity to sensory stimulation (wind, pain, sound, smell, touch)

Severity level for autism spectrum disorder is determined along a continuum, on the basis of degree of impairment for social communication impairments and RRBs separately, according to the following degree:

- Level 1 (requiring support)
- Level 2 (requiring substantial support)
- Level 3 (requiring very substantial support)

Under this new dimensional approach to diagnosis, some people on the autism spectrum show mild symptoms, whereas others have much more severe symptoms (indicated by documentation of Level 3). Interested readers should refer to *DSM-5* for a matrix of severity for autism spectrum disorder (APA, 2013a, p. 52).

A note about Asperger's: The *DSM-5* Childhood and Adolescent Disorders Work Group recommended the use of dimensions of severity instead of a separate diagnosis for Asperger's disorder. Subsuming Asperger's disorder into the overall autism spectrum has been one of the most, if not *the* most, controversial change in *DSM-5*. According to the American Psychiatric Association, the decision was made after conducting considerable research on diagnostic criteria, outcomes, course, etiology, neurocognitive profile, and treatment, among others. Concerns raised by this change include the possibility of increased stigma as people with Asperger's are conceptualized as being on the autism spectrum. Conversely, increased services may now be available to meet the needs of children and adults who in the past may have been denied services because they did not meet the diagnostic criteria set down in *DSM-IV*. The complete impact of the change to a dimensional assessment approach based on verbal language abilities, social interaction, intelligence, and independent living capacity may prove to be a positive change, particularly for children. It seems possible that adults who were previously diagnosed with Asperger's may not benefit as much, although the *DSM-5* also clearly states that "Individuals with a well-established *DSM-IV* diagnosis of autistic disorder, Asperger's disorder, or pervasive developmental disorder not otherwise specified should be given the diagnosis of autism spectrum disorder" (APA, 2013a, p. 51). (See also *DSM-5* Childhood and Adolescent Disorders Work Group, 2010; Frazier et al., 2012; Mao & Yen, 2010.) The grandfathering clause, however, will not help those who are diagnosed in the future. Recent research indicates that the new ASD criteria tends to underdiagnose individuals with symptoms in the milder range of the spectrum.

Following is an example of how an autism spectrum disorder might be coded:

299.00 [F84.0] Autism Spectrum Disorder, requiring substantial support for deficits in social communication and requiring support for restricted repetitive behaviors, without accompanying intellectual impairment, without language impairment.

The differential diagnosis for autism spectrum disorder rules out Rett syndrome, which may share some of the same symptoms as autism spectrum disorder, but not all. If RRBs are absent, social communication disorder would be diagnosed rather than autism spectrum disorder.

Attention-Deficit/Hyperactivity Disorder (ADHD)

The *DSM-5* diagnostic criteria for ADHD recognizes lifespan differences in presentation of ADHD among adults and children and adolescents. Twenty years of research indicates that many adults have the symptoms of ADHD, even though they might not have been diagnosed in childhood. The criteria are calibrated somewhat differently for adults, with the cutoff for symptoms for adult diagnosis of ADHD set at five symptoms rather than the six symptoms required for a younger person. The requirement for onset of symptoms prior to the age of 7 has been loosened to require that five impulsive, inattentive, or hyperactive symptoms were present before the age of 12 (APA, 2013a). Other changes in the *DSM-5* section on ADHD include the provision of adult examples and the requirement that several symptoms must be found in each setting. Eighteen symptoms are provided, along with the requirement that at least six symptoms in either inattention or hyperactivity/impulsivity must be observed for diagnosis. Additional changes include the following:

- ADHD subtypes are now referred to as specifiers.
- A co-occurring diagnosis with autism spectrum disorder is now allowed.
- The cutoff for symptoms for adult diagnosis of ADHD is set at five symptoms rather than the six symptoms required for a younger person.

The prevalence of ADHD in adults is 4.4%. A recent longitudinal study published in the journal *Pediatrics* found that 30% of adults who were diagnosed with ADHD as children continued to have the disorder at the age of 27. Other studies have found the rate to be as high as 50%. In addition, the suicide rate for adults who had childhood ADHD was 5 times higher than for adults who did not have childhood ADHD (Barbaresi et al., 2013).

Assessment and treatment options for adult ADHD include cognitive therapy in conjunction with medication management, when ADHD symptoms are in the moderate to severe range (Montano, 2004).

Specific Learning Disorder

DSM-5 broadens the *DSM-IV* criteria to embrace distinct disorders that impede the acquisition of one or more of the following academic skills: oral language, reading, written language, or mathematics. For each disorder, the severity level of mild, moderate, or severe must be specified.

Motor Disorders

Developmental coordination disorder, stereotypic movement disorder, and tic disorders have been subsumed under the broader category of Motor Disorders in *DSM-5*. Coded specifiers for each type of disorder are included, along with diagnostic criteria, prevalence rates, and differential diagnosis. The tic criteria have been standardized across all of the disorders in the *DSM-5* chapter on neurodevelopmental disorders. Stereotypic movement disorder has been more clearly differentiated from body-focused repetitive behavior disorders that are listed in the *DSM-5* chapter on obsessive-compulsive disorders.

We now move from the neurodevelopmental disorders to a new chapter in *DSM-5*, Schizophrenia Spectrum and Other Psychotic Disorders.

SCHIZOPHRENIA SPECTRUM AND OTHER PSYCHOTIC DISORDERS

DSM-5 takes a spectrum approach to schizophrenia and other psychotic disorders, with all of the disorders being defined by the presence of one or more of the following five domains: (1) delusions, (2) hallucinations, (3) disorganized thinking (or speech), (4) disorganized or abnormal motor behavior, and (5) negative symptoms. Persons are diagnosed on the spectrum according to the number and degree of deficits, ranging from schizotypal personality disorder characterized by odd and eccentric symptoms but without breaks with reality, to schizophrenia, in which hallucinations and delusions are prominent. The presence or absence of mood symptoms along with psychosis informs the diagnosis and has prognostic value in terms of course and treatment considerations.

The relocation of these disorders near the beginning of the *DSM-5* indicates the strong relationships with neurocognitive disorders and the likelihood of a strong genetic link among the psychotic disorders. Readers need to be aware of some small changes that impact the diagnosis of psychotic disorders in the schizophrenia spectrum, although treatment recommendations remain the same.

The following list provides an outline for the new *DSM-5* chapter on Schizophrenia Spectrum and Other Psychotic Disorders. For consistency throughout the text, the *ICD-9* codes are listed first, followed by the diagnosis, and ending with the ICD-10 codes (which often begin with the letter F). A detailed explanation of changes and the implications for assessment, diagnosis, and treatment follows.

ICD CODES AND *DSM* SPECIFIERS

SCHIZOPHRENIA SPECTRUM AND OTHER PSYCHOTIC DISORDERS

ICD-9-CM Code	Diagnosis	ICD-10-CM Code
301.22	Schizotypal (Personality) Disorder	F21
297.1	Delusional Disorder	F22
298.8	Brief Psychotic Disorder	F23
295.40	Schizophreniform Disorder	F20.81
295.90	Schizophrenia	F20.9
295.70	Schizoaffective Disorder, Bipolar type	F25.0
295.70	Schizoaffective Disorder, Depressive type	F25.1
__.__	Substance/Medication-Induced Psychotic Disorder	__.__
	Coding Note: See substance-specific *ICD-9-CM* and *ICD-10-CM* codes and specify if onset is during intoxication or during withdrawal.	
__.__	Psychotic Disorder Due to Another Medical Condition, specify:	__.__
293.81	With Delusions	F06.2
293.82	With Hallucinations	F06.0
293.89	Catatonia Associated with Another Mental Disorder	F06.1
293.89	Catatonic Disorder Due to Another Medical Condition	F06.1
293.89	Unspecified Catatonia	F06.1
298.8	Other Specified Schizophrenia Spectrum and Other Psychotic Disorder	F28
298.9	Unspecified Schizophrenia Spectrum and Other Psychotic Disorder	F29

Schizotypal (Personality) Disorder

Considered to be on the mild side of the schizophrenia spectrum, schizotypal personality disorder is listed in this chapter in *DSM-5*, although the criteria and text remain in the chapter on personality disorders. No changes have been made to the criteria for schizotypal personality disorder from *DSM-IV*.

Delusional Disorder

A hallmark of this disorder is the presence of a delusion without marked impairment in areas of functioning. Indeed, persons with delusional disorder may appear to be quite normal in appearance and behavior, until they begin to discuss their delusional ideas. In *DSM-5*, "with bizarre content" is now a course specifier, and the requirement that delusions must be nonbizarre has been lifted. Differential diagnosis is aided by new exclusion criteria stating that symptoms must not be better explained by conditions such as an obsessive-compulsive disorder or body dysmorphic disorder with absent insight/delusional beliefs (APA, 2013a). Shared delusional disorder (pas de deux) has been eliminated from *DSM-5*. If the diagnosis meets the criteria for delusional disorder, then that diagnosis is made. If the criteria for delusional disorder are not met but shared beliefs are present, then the diagnosis would be other specified schizophrenia spectrum and other psychotic disorder.

Brief Psychotic Disorder and Schizophreniform Disorder

Sudden onset of psychotic symptoms with return to normal within a month is considered to be a brief psychotic disorder. If the disorder continues for 1 month or longer, another schizophrenia spectrum disorder should be considered such as schizophreniform disorder or delusional disorder. Both disorders share the same diagnostic criteria as schizophrenia and generally differ only in terms of duration.

Schizophrenia

Two major changes have been made in the criteria for the diagnosis of schizophrenia. The first is the elimination of two symptoms in Criterion A that were found to have poor reliability and nonspecificity (e.g., bizarre delusions and Schneiderian first-rank auditory hallucinations). Instead, *DSM-5* now requires two symptoms from Criterion A to be present for the diagnosis of schizophrenia. In addition, the person must have at least one of the following core positive symptoms: delusions, hallucinations, or disorganized speech.

The subtypes of schizophrenia have also been removed. It is no longer necessary to distinguish among the paranoid, disorganized, undifferentiated and residual, or catatonic types. These distinctions were found to be lacking in diagnostic stability, reliability, and validity, and were not predictive of treatment response or longitudinal course. Instead, DSM-5 offers a dimensional approach to schizophrenia and the psychotic disorders that allows clinicians to rate severity of core symptoms and discern client behavior on a spectrum (see rating scale on pages 742–744 of DSM-5).

A note about Attenuated Psychosis Syndrome: It is a well-known fact that early diagnosis and treatment of symptoms of psychosis improve long-term prognosis. To encourage earlier identification, Attenuated Psychosis Syndrome was considered for inclusion in the manual. However, the benefits of adding a disorder like this must be balanced with consideration of any possible negative effects of early treatment, such as stigma or overprescription of antipsychotics. DSM-5 Section III, subsection: Conditions for Further Study includes conditions that, with further research, may become full-blown disorders in future updates of the DSM-5. One of the proposed criteria sets provides symptoms and diagnostic features of attenuated psychosis, which usually first appears in adolescents and young adults.

Schizoaffective Disorder

This disorder has long been considered to be a bridge between a bipolar or mood disorder and schizophrenia, with people having symptoms of depression or mania as well as psychotic symptoms. These symptoms may occur concurrently or at different points in the duration of the disorder. DSM-5 now looks at schizoaffective disorder longitudinally, across the course and duration of the disorder, and clarifies that a mood disorder must remain for "most of the time" after Criterion A of schizophrenia (e.g., negative symptoms, delusions, hallucinations) has been met. This new criteria in DSM-5 should improve the clinician's ability to make an accurate differential diagnosis that rules out schizophrenia or a bipolar or depressive disorder.

Catatonia

Although catatonia is no longer a subtype of schizophrenia, DSM-5 allows for catatonia to be included as a specifier for any psychotic, bipolar, or depressive disorder; as a separate diagnosis in the context of another medical condition; or as another unspecified disorder. The criteria remain the same as in DSM-IV. A major difference in DSM-5 is that all contexts require the presence of three catatonic symptoms out of a total of 12 possible symptoms (e.g., waxy flexibility, negativism, posturing, mimicking others' speech or movements, lack of response, agitation, grimacing, repetitive movements, catalepsy, stupor).

* * *

BIPOLAR AND RELATED DISORDERS

The diagnosis and treatment of mood disorders has been refined in *DSM-5* by dividing the mood disorders into two distinct chapters: a chapter on bipolar and related disorders (bipolar I and II, cyclothymic disorder, and four new disorders) and a chapter on depressive disorders. Disruptive mood dysregulation disorder (DMDD) is a new diagnosis for children under the age of 18 who present with extreme emotional and behavioral dysregulation. Its description is included in the chapter on depressive disorders, since most children with this symptom profile do not go on to develop bipolar disorder. Rather, a depressive disorder or anxiety disorder is more likely to develop in adulthood.

ICD CODES AND *DSM* SPECIFIERS

BIPOLAR AND RELATED DISORDERS

ICD-9-CM Code	Diagnosis	ICD-10-CM Code
__.__	Bipolar I Disorder: Current or most recent episode manic, specify:	__.__
296.41	Mild	F31.11
296.42	Moderate	F31.12
296.43	Severe, without psychotic features	F31.13
296.44	Severe, with psychotic features	F31.2
296.45	In partial remission	F31.73
296.46	In full remission	F31.74
296.40	Unspecified	F31.9
296.40	Bipolar I Disorder: Current or most recent episode hypomanic, specify	F31.0
296.45	In partial remission	F31.71
296.46	In full remission	F31.72
296.40	Unspecified	F31.9

ICD-9-CM Code	Diagnosis	ICD-10-CM Code
__.__	Bipolar I Disorder: Current or most recent episode depressed, specify	__.__
296.51	Mild	F31.31
296.52	Moderate	F31.32
296.53	Severe, without psychotic features	F31.4
296.54	Severe, with psychotic features	F31.5
296.55	In partial remission	F31.75
296.56	In full remission	F31.76
296.50	Unspecified	F31.9
296.7	Bipolar I Disorder: Current or most recent episode unspecified	F31.9
296.89	Bipolar II Disorder	F31.81

Coding Note: Specify for most recent episode, either hypomanic or depressed
Specify course if full criteria for a mood episode are not currently met: In partial remission, In full remission
Specify severity if full criteria for a mood episode are not currently met: Mild, Moderate, Severe

301.13	Cyclothymic Disorder	F34.0

Specify if with anxious distress

__.__	Substance/Medication-Induced Bipolar and Related Disorder	__.__

Coding Note: See substance-specific codes and ICD-9-CM and ICD-10-CM coding.
Specify if: onset is during intoxication, onset is during withdrawal

293.83	Bipolar and Related Disorder Due to Another Medical Condition (indicate condition), specify:	
	With manic features	F06.33
	With manic- or hypomanic-like episode	F06.33
	With mixed features	F06.34
296.89	Other Specified Bipolar and Related Disorder	F31.89
296.80	Unspecified Bipolar and Related Disorder	F31.9

We now turn to a detailed look at each of the bipolar disorders.

Bipolar I, Bipolar II, and Cyclothymia

DSM-5 includes six pages of course specifiers for bipolar and related disorders. Many specifiers are the same as in DSM-IV (e.g., "with rapid cycling," "with seasonal pattern"). New specifiers have been made in the bipolar disorders in DSM-5 to facilitate earlier and more accurate diagnosis. Diagnosis of mania has been enhanced with the inclusion of changes in "activity and energy level," not just changes in mood. A new specifier "with mixed features" replaces the mixed episode criterion that was found in DSM-IV. The specifier can be applied to episodes of depression (in either MDD or bipolar disorders) when features of mania or hypomania are present, or to hypomania or mania when depressive features are present. The distinction is that the "mixed episode" specifier in DSM-IV required the person to meet the full criteria for both mania and a major depressive episode concurrently. That is no longer the case.

Other Bipolar Disorders

There are many variations of bipolar disorder, in addition to bipolar I, bipolar II, and cyclothymia. Bipolar disorder NOS was a frequently used diagnosis in DSM-IV that has been replaced with the following four diagnoses to specify the appropriate type of bipolar disorder that is being presented:

- Substance/medication-induced bipolar and related disorder
- Bipolar and related disorder due to another medical condition
- Other specified bipolar and related disorder
- Unspecified bipolar and related disorder

Readers are reminded that, in children, a diagnosis of disruptive mood dysregulation disorder (which is discussed later) is generally more appropriate than the diagnosis of bipolar disorder.

Substance/medication-induced bipolar and related disorder would be the appropriate diagnosis if evidence suggests that the symptoms of bipolar disorder occurred during or soon after substance intoxication or withdrawal, or after the exposure to a medication that is known to produce the symptoms of bipolar disorder. In such situations, the substance ingested would be listed, along with a specifier indicating whether onset was during intoxication or during withdrawal.

Bipolar and related disorder due to another medical condition would be the appropriate diagnosis if the manic, hypomanic, or mixed symptoms occur as a direct pathophysiological result of another medical condition. The medical conditions most commonly associated with the development of a bipolar disorder are Cushing's disease, hyperthyroidism, lupus, multiple sclerosis, stroke, and traumatic brain injury (APA, 2013a).

Other specified and unspecified bipolar and related disorder refers to the presentation of symptoms of a bipolar disorder that do not meet the full criteria, but in which distress in social, occupational, or other areas of functioning is present. Insufficient information may be available, or the clinician may choose not to specify the reason why the criteria were not met.

Anxious Distress Specifier

Anxious distress is a new specifier to be considered in all mood disorders, including bipolar and related disorders. Anxious distress refers to persons exhibiting anxiety symptoms beyond the diagnostic criteria for a mood episode (manic, hypomanic, or depressed). Following is a description of the anxious distress specifier that is applicable to bipolar disorders and depressive disorders.

To qualify for the anxious distress specifier, a minimum of two of the following anxiety symptoms must be present most days during the current or most recent mood episode of mania, hypomania, or depression (APA, 2013a):

- tension or feeling wound up
- restlessness
- inability to concentrate
- dread of something terrible happening
- fear of losing control

Severity levels—mild (two symptoms), moderate (three symptoms), moderate-severe (four or five symptoms), or severe (four or five symptoms with motor agitation)—should be assessed for anxious distress.

A great deal of research indicates that the presence of anxiety in conjunction with depression can be destabilizing and may potentially increase the risk of suicidality, longer duration of illness, or lack of response to treatment. Thus, the anxious distress specifier must be accurately assessed, along with additional assessment of suicidal risk factors, including potential plans, thoughts, or history, in persons who exhibit moderate to severe levels of anxious distress. Suicide assessment should also be kept in mind when making a diagnosis of major depressive disorder, to which we now turn.

DEPRESSIVE DISORDERS

The *DSM-5* chapter on depressive disorders includes two new disorders: (1) premenstrual dysphoric disorder (previously in the Appendix of *DSM-IV*) and (2) disruptive mood dysregulation disorder (DMDD), which is specific to children who present with extreme irritability and emotional dysregulation.

Depression is conceptualized in a new way. Dysthymia has been combined with chronic major depressive disorder and is now referred to as persistent depressive disorder. Also new in *DSM-5* is the elimination of the bereavement exclusion criterion from the diagnosis of major depressive disorder. Following is a list of depressive disorders, and their codes, followed by a more detailed explanation of specific changes from *DSM-IV* to *DSM-5*.

ICD CODES AND *DSM* SPECIFIERS

DEPRESSIVE DISORDERS

ICD-9-CM Code	Diagnosis	ICD-10-CM Code
296.99	Disruptive Mood Dysregulation Disorder	F34.8
__.__	Major Depressive Disorder	__.__
__.__	Single episode	__.__
296.21	Mild	F32.0
296.22	Moderate	F32.1
296.23	Severe	F32.2
296.24	With psychotic features	F32.3
296.25	In partial remission	F32.4
296.26	In full remission	F32.5
296.20	Unspecified	F32.9
__.__	Recurrent episode	__.__
296.31	Mild	F33.0
296.32	Moderate	F33.1
296.33	Severe	F33.2
296.34	With psychotic features	F33.3
296.35	In partial remission	F33.41
296.36	In full remission	F33.42
296.30	Unspecified	F33.9
300.4	Persistent Depressive Disorder (Dysthymia)	F34.1

Specify if: In partial remission, In full remission
Early onset, late onset
With pure dysthymic syndrome; with persistent major depressive episode; with intermittent major depressive episodes, with current episode or without current episode

ICD-9-CM Code	Diagnosis	ICD-10-CM Code
625.4	Premenstrual Dysphoric Disorder	N94.3
__.__	Substance/Medication-Induced Depressive Disorder	__.__

Coding Note: See substance-specific codes and *ICD-9-CM* and *ICD-10-CM* coding.
Specify if: onset is during intoxication, onset is during withdrawal

ICD-9-CM Code	Diagnosis	ICD-10-CM Code
293.83	Depressive Disorder Due to Another Medical Condition	__.__
	With depressive features	F06.31
	With major depressive-like episode	F06.32
	With mixed features	F06.34
311	Other Specified Depressive Disorder	F32.8
311	Unspecified Depressive Disorder	F32.9

Disruptive Mood Dysregulation Disorder

Temper or anger outbursts with underlying persistent irritability dispropor-tionate to the situation and unrelenting over a 12-month period is the hallmark feature of disruptive mood dysregulation disorder, a new *DSM-5* disorder that affects children over the age of 6.

The intent of this disorder is to distinguish children with the milder DMDD from the diagnosis of childhood-onset bipolar disorder. Overall, research does not indicate that the preponderance of children diagnosed and treated for bipolar disorder actually go on to develop bipolar disorder as adults. In fact, longitudinal studies indicate that the majority of children treated for symp-toms of intense irritability and disruptive behavior actually develop unipolar depression or anxiety disorders as young adults. In effect, bipolar disorder occurs in less than 1% of children before the onset of puberty. Because little research is available on the long-term effects of psychotropic medications on young brains that are not fully developed, the intent of identifying this disorder is to reduce the number of such prescriptions that are given to young children. For a complete discussion of both sides of the controversy surrounding the diagnosis of bipolar disorder in children, refer to Leibenluft (2011) and Wash-burn, West, and Heil (2011).

The symptoms of DMDD include the following:

- Severe chronic temper outbursts, verbal aggression, or emotional storms that are out of proportion to the situation.
- The outbursts occur an average of three or more times per week.
- They occur for a period of 12 or more months.
- Persistent irritability does not remit when stressors go away, or between episodes, and is observable by others (e.g., friends, family, teachers).
- Irritability is observed in at least two out of three settings (home, school, with peers) and is severe in at least one of these locations.
- The diagnosis can not be made prior to the age of 6, nor after the age of 18.
- Historical assessment finds that these symptoms were present prior to the age of 10.
- There has been no prior diagnosis of a mania or euphoric mood lasting longer than 1 day.
- The behaviors do not occur as a result of a major depressive or other disorder, such as anxiety, persistent depressive disorder, or posttraumatic stress disorder.
- The disorder is not better accounted for by a bipolar disorder, a substance, or a medical or neurological condition (APA, 2013a).

DMDD is a severe disorder. Approximately 50% of children who present with these symptoms will continue to have chronic irritability 1 year later. The behavior is extreme enough to cause disruption in peer and family relationships, difficulties in school, and problems maintaining relationships. Dangerous behaviors such as aggression, suicide attempts, and self-harming are common, as is hospitalization. The presence of co-occurring disorders is also high, so careful assessment is necessary to distinguish DMDD from childhood-onset bipolar disorder, oppositional defiant disorder, ADHD, and intermittent explosive disorder. Oppositional defiant disorder is most frequently comorbid with DMDD. Intermittent explosive disorder, which has a duration of 3 months, with remittance between episodes, should not be diagnosed concurrently with DMDD, which has a 12-month minimum duration and remains persistent over the 12-month period.

The behavior must also be inconsistent with the child's age and developmental level and cannot be better explained by autism spectrum disorder, PTSD, or pervasive developmental disabilities. If the child has already been diagnosed with bipolar disorder, intermittent explosive disorder, or oppositional defiant disorder, a diagnosis of DMDD would not be appropriate (APA, 2013a).

Major Depressive Disorder

With two exceptions, the diagnosis and treatment of the classic major depressive disorder remains the same as described in *DSM-IV*. The exceptions are the addition of new specifiers (described later) and the elimination of the bereavement exclusion, which we address next.

The Bereavement Exclusion

A major change in the diagnosis of major depressive disorder is the removal of the bereavement exclusion, which prevented a person who was grieving from being diagnosed with major depressive disorder in the first 2 months following the death of a loved one. Under the old *DSM-IV* criteria, a person would have been considered to be grieving rather than depressed. APA research teams discovered, however, that persons who had experienced a major depressive episode prior to a major loss were far more likely to have a recurrent depressive episode after a loss, and the bereavement exclusion was preventing them from being accurately diagnosed and receiving the appropriate care. Second, removal of the bereavement exclusion is an acknowledgment of the fact that grief does not end after only 2 months. Grief is a far more complicated process that must take into account multiple factors, including relationship, age, and cause of death. Grieving the loss of a spouse after 50 years of marriage, for example, may never be resolved, and certainly not within the 2-month period allotted for grief.

    DSM-5 actually expands the caution about diagnosing MDE to include any significant loss (e.g., divorce, financial ruin, natural disasters, loss of children through custody disputes) that causes intense sadness, insomnia, inability to eat, and rumination. Even though the symptoms may be appropriate to the loss, the presence of a major depressive episode must still be ruled out, especially in individuals with a prior history of a depressive disorder. When making a diagnosis, clinicians should also consider cultural norms related to the expression of grief and loss.

    DSM-5 includes a comprehensive footnote (APA, 2013a, p. 161) to clarify the purpose of the bereavement exclusion and to help clinicians distinguish between symptoms of grief and loss and the presence of a major depressive episode (MDE), while also understanding that both may be present. When grief occurs in conjunction with an MDE, symptoms may be more severe and poorer outcomes may result, including increased risk for suicidality and risk of developing persistent complex bereavement disorder, a Condition for Further Study, which can be found in *DSM-5* Section III: Emerging Measures and Models.

New Specifiers
As described earlier in the bipolar disorders section, an "anxious distress" specifier has been added in *DSM-5* for all depressive disorders, and the specifier "with mixed features" allows for the possibility of manic features in a person who has been diagnosed with unipolar depression.

Persistent Depressive Disorder (Dysthymia)

Dysthymic disorder, which appeared in *DSM-IV*, has been combined with chronic major depressive disorder to create this broader category of persistent depressive disorder. The hallmark of this disorder is a depressed mood that lasts most of the day, for most days, over a 2-year period (1 year for children and adolescents). The chronicity of this disorder can be identified through the use of course specifiers, which are similar to those for major depressive disorder. Risk factors for childhood-onset PDD include parental loss or separation. The early-onset specifier is given if the disorder is diagnosed prior to the age of 21.

Premenstrual Dysphoric Disorder

Decades of research have confirmed that premenstrual dysphoric disorder (PMDD) is a specific and treatment-responsive form of depressive disorder that occurs in a small number of women. Specifically, it has been estimated that 75% of women experience minor symptoms premenstrually, with 20% to 30% experiencing the less severe premenstrual syndrome, which does not require the presence of five criteria or changes in affect. Only 2% to 10% of premenopausal women, however, are expected to meet the criteria for the more severe PMDD (Epperson et al., 2012). Research indicates that PMDD is separate from a mood disorder (although it can occur in conjunction with one). Mood lability and irritability are the primary symptoms, and must be present most months in the previous 12-month period, appearing in the week before the onset of menses, start to improve after menses begins, and recede postmenses. Criterion D requires clinically significant distress. The criteria for PMDD are slightly more stringent than those that appeared in the Appendix to *DSM-IV*, requiring 5 of the following 11 symptoms to be necessary for diagnosis:

1. Feelings of hopelessness, sadness, or low self-esteem
2. Feeling tense or anxious
3. Emotional lability that includes tearfulness

4. Irritability, often accompanied by increased interpersonal conflict
5. Difficulty concentrating
6. Tiredness, lethargy, or lack of energy
7. Changes in appetite, cravings, or binge eating
8. Decreased interest in activities
9. Sleep disturbances—oversleeping or insomnia
10. Feelings of being overwhelmed
11. Headaches, bloating, breast tenderness, or other physical symptoms

Symptoms may be as severe as major depressive disorder, although lasting for less than a week. The symptoms must cause clinically significant distress or marked disruption in relationships and/or social or occupational functioning during the affected week.

Assessment of PMDD begins by charting symptoms prospectively for a 2-month period to confirm the presence of a cyclical pattern. The chart should be maintained daily and may include self-report and/or input from a person who lives with the woman.

PMDD must be distinguished from mental disorders that are made worse premenstrually. The symptoms cannot be a result of medication or substance use, nor an exacerbation of a current medical condition (e.g., hyperthyroidism). If oral contraceptives are used, PMDD cannot be diagnosed unless symptoms continue, and are as severe, when contraceptives are removed. Most cases of PMDD worsen with age and then subside with the onset of menopause (APA, 2013a).

Treatment for PMDD focuses on controlling or minimizing symptoms. Women should not suffer because of fears about stigma. Research has validated that antidepressants and anxiolytics administered during the period between ovulation and onset of menses have been shown to reduce emotionality and other symptoms. Selective serotonin reuptake inhibitors are considered to be the first line of treatment for PMDD (Cunningham, Yonkers, O'Brien, & Eriksson, 2009). Medications that suppress ovulation have also been shown to be effective for some women, although they can have a rebound effect (Epperson et al., 2012). Vitamins and supplements such as vitamin B_6, calcium, and magnesium have been shown to help in some studies, but more research is necessary. In general, treatments that help with other mood disorders can also be effective with PMDD: herbal remedies (to reduce irritability, mood swings, and headaches), aerobic exercise to improve mood and energy; lifestyle changes such as relaxation; and cognitive therapy to help reduce stress (Pearlstein & Steiner, 2008).

Substance/Medication-Induced Depressive Disorder

The use of alcohol or illicit drugs can result in the development of depression while using the substance or during the withdrawal period. Similarly, many medications prescribed to treat physical and psychological conditions, including antidepressants, may also have the untoward side effect of causing depression (APA, 2013a). Antidepressants are generally considered safe, but the suicide risk for young adults ages 18 to 24 who begin taking antidepressants was large enough for the Food and Drug Administration to issue a black-box warning to advocate careful monitoring of clients in this age group for treatment-emergent suicidal ideation (Friedman & Leon, 2007; Seligman & Reichenberg, 2012).

Depressive Disorder Due to Another Medical Condition

Stroke, Parkinson's disease, Huntington's disease, lupus, and Cushing's disease are all illnesses that have been linked with depression. Some symptoms may be episodic and may go away after the medical disorder is treated. There is also a clear connection between some severe medical disorders and suicide, especially in the weeks following the initial diagnosis.

Other Specified Depressive Disorder

When criteria for a specific depressive disorder are not completely met, one of the following designations can be considered: recurrent brief depression (does not meet the duration criterion), short-duration depressive episode (in situations without a prior history of mood disorder), and depressive episode with insufficient symptoms (depressed affect and at least one other symptom). For example, a person who presents with a minimum of 2 weeks of clinically significant distress, depressed affect and at least one of the eight symptoms of a MDE would be coded as:

> 311 [F32.8] Other Specified Depressive Disorder, depressive episode with insufficient symptoms

Unspecified Depressive Disorder

This diagnosis is given when depression is present and causes significant problems in social, occupational, or other important areas of functioning, but does not meet the full criteria for any of the depressive disorders listed earlier, and the clinician does not wish to specify or does not have enough information to give a more specific diagnosis.

Additional Specifiers for Depressive Disorders

DSM-5 maintains all of the specifiers for depressive disorder that were found in *DSM-IV* (e.g., "with melancholic features," "with atypical features," "with psychotic features," "with catatonia," "with paripartum onset," "with seasonal pattern," "in partial remission," "in full remission," and specifiers of severity. As mentioned earlier in the discussion of bipolar disorders, *DSM-5* also adds an "anxious distress" specifier to all mood disorders, along with an assessment of current severity level.

ANXIETY DISORDERS

The former Anxiety Disorders of *DSM-IV* have been redistributed into three consecutive classifications in *DSM-5*: Anxiety Disorders, Obsessive-Compulsive and Related Disorders, and Trauma- and Stressor-Related Disorders. The Anxiety Disorders section includes disorders that have the same shared features of excessive fear and anxiety along with behavioral disturbances. The creation of a new classification of Obsessive-Compulsive and Related Disorders reflects emerging evidence of the relatedness of disorders such as OCD, hoarding, and body dysmorphic disorder, among others. The third chapter, Trauma- and Stressor-Related Disorders, includes disorders that result from exposure to a stressful or traumatic event. More will be said about this later.

Now we turn to the *DSM-5* chapter related to anxiety disorders, which now includes the following list of disorders. Readers will note that in keeping with the developmental lifespan approach of *DSM-5*, several disorders that were previously located in the children's section of *DSM-IV* (e.g., separation anxiety disorder and selective mutism) have been reclassified as anxiety disorders, although the criteria remain much the same.

Minimal changes have been made to the criteria for the diagnosis of anxiety disorders, with the exception of separate criteria for agoraphobia and panic disorder and the addition of a "performance only" specifier for social anxiety disorder. The criteria for agoraphobia, specific phobia, and social anxiety disorder no longer require that the person recognize that the anxiety is unreasonable or excessive. Instead, and after accounting for cultural context, the anxiety must be out of proportion to the actual danger or threat imposed by the situation. The requirement of a 6-month duration is now extended to all ages in *DSM-5*, with the intent of reducing the overdiagnosis of short-lived fears or anxieties.

We turn now to a list of anxiety disorders and their codes followed by highlights of the changes included in *DSM-5*.

ICD CODES AND DSM SPECIFIERS

ANXIETY DISORDERS

ICD-9-CM Code	Diagnosis	ICD-10-CM Code
309.21	Separation Anxiety Disorder	F93
313.23	Selective Mutism	F94.0
300.29	Specific Phobia	
ICD-10-CM codes are based on the specific phobia type, as follows:		
	Animal (e.g., rats, spiders)	F40.218
	Natural environment (e.g., heights, storms)	F40.228
	Blood-injection-injury	
	ICD-10-CM requires specification of:	
	Fear of blood	F40.230
	Fear of injections and transfusions	F40.231
	Fear of other medical care	F40.232
	Fear of injury	F40.233
300.29	Situational (e.g., enclosed places, elevators, airplanes)	F40.248
300.29	Other (e.g., in children—loud sounds, balloons, or costumed characters; situations that may lead to vomiting or choking)	F40.298
300.23	Social Anxiety Disorder (formerly social phobia) Specify if performance only	F40.10
300.01	Panic Disorder Panic attack (used as a specifier)	F41.0
300.22	Agoraphobia	F40.00
300.02	Generalized Anxiety Disorder	F41.1
__.__	Substance/Medication-Induced Anxiety Disorder	__.__
Coding Note: See substance-specific codes and ICD-9-CM and ICD-10-CM coding. Specify if: With onset during intoxication, With onset during withdrawal, With onset after medication use		
293.84	Anxiety Disorder Due to Another Medical Condition (indicate condition)	F06.4
300.09	Other Specified Anxiety Disorder	F41.8
300.00	Unspecified Anxiety Disorder	F41.9

Separation Anxiety Disorder

The hallmark of separation anxiety disorder is the presence of excessive fear or anxiety regarding separation from attachment figures. Once considered the domain of childhood, separation anxiety disorder can now be coded in adults. Since the criteria for childhood onset of this disorder remains the same as DSM-IV, this section focuses specifically on adult presentation of this condition, which is frequently comorbid with generalized anxiety disorder and may severely limit a person's ability to travel, or work outside of the home.

The prevalence rate of separation anxiety disorder decreases across the lifespan, from a high of 4% in childhood to 1% to 2% of adults. Symptoms also vary by developmental stage. Adults may be dependent and overprotective and may experience cardiovascular symptoms (e.g., palpitations, dizziness, feeling faint) that are rarely seen in children. Whereas children may express school refusal or concerns about leaving home, adults with the disorder tend to exhibit fear of change, or be overly concerned about being separated from their children or from significant others.

The duration criteria specifies that the anxiety must last a minimum of 4 weeks in children and adolescents, and 6 months or more in adults. It is also important to differentiate separation anxiety disorder from the high value some cultures place on interdependence among family members (APA, 2013a).

Selective Mutism

Selective mutism has been reclassified in DSM-5 as an anxiety disorder. The criteria for selective mutism remains the same; the only difference is its relocation to this chapter from the DSM-IV category of disorders that are first diagnosed in childhood and adolescence.

Specific Phobia

The core criteria of specific phobias remain largely unchanged, with the addition of the broadbrush criteria change for all anxiety disorders (i.e., minimum 6 months' duration and the deletion of the requirement that the person must recognize that the anxiety is excessive). The specific types of phobias are now considered to be specifiers. Anxiety symptoms of specific phobia in children may include crying, tantrums, freezing, or clinging behaviors.

Social Anxiety Disorder

This was previously referred to as "social phobia." The criteria for *DSM-5* social anxiety disorder remain largely the same, with the adoption of the following changes:

1. Minimum duration of 6 months applies to all ages.
2. The requirement that the person recognize that the fear or anxiety is excessive has been dropped.
3. The "generalized" specifier has been replaced with a "performance only" specifier, in recognition of a distinct subset of social anxiety disorder that relates specifically to people whose anxiety response is specific to public speaking or performing in front of an audience. Age of onset and etiology appear to be different for the "performance only" specifier, which has implications for assessment and treatment recommendations as well.

Panic Disorder

Panic disorder and agoraphobia have been separated in *DSM-5*. Previous options for diagnosis in *DSM-IV* were: panic disorder without agoraphobia, panic disorder with agoraphobia, and agoraphobia without history of panic disorder. *DSM-5* has replaced these diagnoses with two distinct disorders: (1) panic disorder and (2) agoraphobia. Persons with both panic disorder and agoraphobia will now receive two diagnoses. The change was made in recognition of the fact that many people with agoraphobia do not experience symptoms of panic. The diagnostic criteria for agoraphobia now require two or more agoraphobic situations prior to diagnosis, as well as the changes noted earlier (i.e., the anxiety must be of a minimum 6-month duration and determined by the clinician to be excessive).

The essential features of panic disorder remain largely the same, although type descriptions of situationally bound (in anticipation of a specific trigger), situationally predisposed (usually associated with a specific trigger), and unexpected/uncued (unrelated to any obvious trigger) have been simplified into two type descriptions: "unexpected" and "expected." Recurrent panic attacks that occur in conjunction with a thunderstorm, for example, would be "expected."

The feelings of panic are caused by fear and stress, and commonly co-occur in other *DSM-5* disorders as well. Thus, panic attacks can serve as a diagnostic indicator of severity, course, and prognosis across a variety of disorders, and can be listed as a specifier for any *DSM-5* disorder.

Agoraphobia

Agoraphobia has been unlinked from panic disorder and is now a separate diagnosis under *DSM-5*. The criteria for agoraphobia include fear and anxiety of being in public (closed spaces, public transportation), fear of being unable to escape, and avoidance of such situations or requiring a companion. The fear must be persistent (lasting 6 months or more), out of proportion to the danger that is present, and cannot be accounted for by another psychological or medical disorder. If both panic and agoraphobia are present, both would be listed.

* * *

OBSESSIVE-COMPULSIVE AND RELATED DISORDERS

Following the list of disorders and codes for the new *DSM-5* chapter Obsessive-Compulsive and Related Disorders, diagnostic criteria, specifiers, and other information new to *DSM-5* will be provided.

ICD CODES AND *DSM* SPECIFIERS

OBSESSIVE-COMPULSIVE AND RELATED DISORDERS

ICD-9-CM Code	Diagnosis	ICD-10-CM Code
300.3	Obsessive-Compulsive Disorder	F42
300.7	Body Dysmorphic Disorder	F45.22
300.3	Hoarding Disorder	F42
312.39	Trichotillomania (Hair-Pulling Disorder)	F63.3
698.4	Excoriation (Skin-Picking Disorder)	L98.1
__.__	Substance/Medication-Induced Obsessive Compulsive and Related Disorder	__.__

Coding Note: See substance-specific codes and *ICD-9-CM* and *ICD-10-CM* coding.
Specify if: With onset during intoxication, With onset during withdrawal, With onset after medication use

294.8	Obsessive-Compulsive and Related Disorder Due To Another Medical Condition	F06.8
300.3	Other Specified Obsessive-Compulsive and Related Disorder	F42
300.3	Unspecified Obsessive-Compulsive and Related Disorder	F42

Obsessive-compulsive disorder (OCD) has become the 10th leading cause of disability in the developed countries. It seems fitting that this debilitating and chronic disorder is the focus of its own chapter in *DSM-5*. In keeping with the reorganization of *DSM-5* to locate related disorders in the same chapter, body dysmorphic disorder (no longer considered to be a somatoform disorder) and trichotillomania (hair-pulling disorder) have also been moved to this chapter. Two new disorders have been added: hoarding disorder and excoriation (skin-picking disorder), which are discussed at length later. Medication-induced obsessive-compulsive disorder and obsessive-compulsive and related disorder due to another medical condition are also included here.

Obsessive-Compulsive Disorder (OCD)

OCD has been relocated from the anxiety disorders chapter to this new chapter in *DSM-5*. With the exception of a few new specifiers for OCD, the bulk of the criteria remain the same. The specifier "with poor insight" has been expanded in *DSM-5* to provide a range from: good to fair insight, poor insight, or absent insight/delusional. The insight specifier should help improve the differential diagnosis. For example, OCD absent insight/delusional should not be confused with a schizophrenia spectrum or other psychotic disorder. A tic-related specifier has also been added due to the growing acknowledgment of the relationship between tic disorder and the development of OCD.

Body Dysmorphic Disorder

This disorder was previously considered to be one of the somatoform disorders, but it is now more appropriately listed in the OCD family. Most of the criteria remain the same, with the addition of a new criterion to describe repetitive thoughts or behaviors related to preoccupation with perceived defects or flaws in physical appearance. Insight specifiers (fair, poor, absent insight/delusional) have also been added. For example, a person lacking insight who completely believes that the perceived defect or appearance flaw is abnormal or disgusting would be diagnosed with body dysmorphic disorder, absent insight/delusional, instead of the former diagnosis under *DSM-IV* of delusional disorder, somatic type. Treatment strategies remain the same (e.g., habit reversal and exposure and response-prevention training, CBT for milder disorders, and combination therapy with SSRIs for people who present with more severe or delusional symptoms).

Hoarding Disorder

Hoarding behavior was previously a symptom of obsessive-compulsive personality disorder in *DSM-IV*, but it is now considered to be a discrete disorder grounded on research-based evidence of its diagnostic validity and clinical utility (APA, 2013a). This disorder may have distinctive neurobiological correlates and is frequently associated with symptoms such as the accumulation of items and clutter that prevent the normal use of a space (e.g., using the shower as a place to store boxes of clothing). The symptoms must cause significant distress or impairment in areas of functioning and may or may not be associated with excessive acquisition. Insight specifiers (good/fair, poor, or absent insight/delusional) have been determined for hoarding disorder in an effort to improve the differential diagnosis and distinguish people who hoard and lack insight from those who may have a schizophrenia spectrum or other psychotic disorder that results in accumulation of objects because of delusional beliefs.

Hoarding disorder is new to *DSM-5*. The criteria for diagnosis of this new disorder include the following:

- Long-standing problems exist with discarding (including selling, recycling, throwing away, or donating) possessions, even those that have no actual value.
- Saving items is intentional, and feelings of distress (e.g., anxiety, fear of losing important information, loss of emotional attachment to items, fear that the item will be needed later) arise at the thought of discarding the items.
- The large volume of clutter interferes with the use of "active living areas" for the purpose they were intended (e.g., dining room table so cluttered with papers and books that it hasn't been used for dining in months).
- Distress or impairment in social, occupational, or other important areas of functioning must be present. For example, relationships may end because the person does not allow others inside the house because moving from room to room through piles of detritus would be untenable.
- The symptoms of hoarding must not be caused by the presence of a medical condition (e.g., brain injury).
- The disorder is not the result of a separate mental disorder (e.g., OCD, MDD, autism spectrum disorder, or others).

Specifiers for hoarding disorder include:

With excessive acquisition—80% to 90% of people who meet the criteria for this disorder will also display excessive acquisition in addition to difficulty discarding items. Excessive acquisition is defined in *DSM-5* as excessive buying, acquiring items for free (or less commonly stealing), items for which there is no space, or the items are not needed. Distress may be experienced if the person is inhibited from acquiring possessions.

Level of insight—Good or fair, poor, or absent insight/delusional must be specified. Good or fair insight assumes the person is aware that the hoarding behavior is excessive and causes problems. Poor insight is specified if the person mostly believes that hoarding-related behavior is not a problem, despite evidence to the contrary. Absent insight/delusional beliefs would be indicated if the person is convinced the beliefs or behaviors are not a problem.

Hoarding behavior has become increasingly common, affecting 2% to 6% of the population in the United States and Europe. The disorder is nearly 3 times more likely to occur in adults age 55 or older than in younger adults. Hoarding can be distinguished from "collecting," which is organized and intentional and does not result in the clutter, distress, or impairment seen in hoarding disorder. Clutter, a requirement of Criterion C, is defined as: "a large group of usually unrelated or marginally related objects piled together in a disorganized fashion in spaces designed for other purposes" (APA, 2013a, p. 248). Criterion C also emphasizes that the clutter must be present in the active living areas of the home, and not just garages, sheds, basements, or other areas designed for storage. If the lack of clutter is the result of third-party intervention (professionals, family, or authorities), the person is still considered to have a hoarding disorder.

Approximately 50% of persons who develop hoarding disorder have a first-degree relative who hoards. Indecisiveness is a common trait, and many people report that a traumatic or stressful event (such as the death of a loved one) precipitated the development of the disorder. As many as 75% of persons with hoarding disorder have a comorbid mood or anxiety disorder. Only 20% also qualify for a diagnosis of OCD. Hoarding behavior that is the result of a brain injury, neurodevelopmental disorder, or with gradual onset following the diagnosis of a neurocognitive disorder (e.g., Alzheimer's) would not be diagnosed as hoarding disorder.

Cognitive-behavior therapy that focuses on exposure and response prevention (ERT) appears to be the best treatment for hoarding disorder, although many people refuse to participate (Seligman & Reichenberg, 2012, p. 219). Also helpful is cognitive therapy that helps people who hoard to challenge their faulty beliefs (e.g., that possessions are valuable, that they "need" the item), and family involvement in treatment. The use of visualization to imagine success, mindfulness to help reduce negative psychological states, and photographs to measure progress can also be helpful. For a complete discussion of the use of exposure and response-prevention therapy for the treatment of hoarding disorder, refer to Seligman and Reichenberg (2013).

Trichotillomania (Hair-Pulling Disorder)

The only changes from *DSM-IV* are the parenthetical inclusion of the words *hair-pulling disorder* to the name, and its relocation from the behavior and impulse-control disorders to the chapter on obsessive-compulsive disorders. The criteria for this disorder has not changed from *DSM-IV*.

Excoriation (Skin-Picking Disorder)

Recurrent skin-picking, most commonly on the arms, face, and hands, is the focus of a new disorder in *DSM-5*. Excoriation affects 1.4% of the population and is more common in persons with obsessive-compulsive disorder and their first-degree family members. This disorder is highly gender specific, with females constituting 75% of the people affected. Although onset may occur at any age, most frequently it coincides with the onset of puberty and may begin with a dermatological condition such as acne, and may increase in time spent and rituals. Specific criteria for excoriation (skin-picking disorder) are:

- The presence of recurrent skin picking that results in lesions.
- Repeated attempts to stop skin picking must have been made.
- Distress or impairment in social, occupational or other important areas of functioning must be present. Distress may also include embarrassment, shame, and other emotions that result from the skin picking.
- The symptoms of skin picking must not be caused by the use of a drug or as the result of a medical condition.
- The disorder is not better accounted for by a separate mental disorder (e.g., delusions or hallucinations that lead the person to pick the skin during a psychotic episode).

This disorder is highly comorbid with OCD, trichotillomania, and major depressive disorder. It may also coincide with other specified obsessive-compulsive and related disorders, such as body-focused repetitive behavior disorders (e.g., nail-biting, lip-chewing), which should also be considered. Skin-picking must be differentiated from nonsuicidal self-injury. If excoriation or skin-picking is primarily intended to cause self-harm, it would not be diagnosed as excoriation and may be better accounted for by nonsuicidal self-injury.

Substance/Medication-Induced Obsessive-Compulsive and Related Disorder and Obsessive-Compulsive and Related Disorder Due to Another Medical Condition

Both of these disorders were added to this chapter on OCD in recognition of the fact that many anxiety disorders listed in *DSM-IV* included the specifier "with obsessive-compulsive symptoms." In other words, this disorder reflects the reality that some medications, substances, or medical conditions can induce symptoms similar to obsessive-compulsive and related disorders. If obsessive-compulsive and related disorder due to another medical condition is diagnosed, specify if: with OCD-like symptoms; with appearance preoccupations; with hoarding symptoms; with hair-pulling symptoms, or with skin-picking symptoms.

Other Specified Obsessive-Compulsive and Related Disorders

This category applies to symptoms that are similar to OCD but do not meet the full criteria. Examples provided in *DSM-5* include, but are not limited to, the following:

1. Body-dysmorphic-like disorder with actual flaws: Preoccupation with real flaws in physical appearance. The preoccupation becomes obsessive and interferes with daily functioning.
2. Body dysmorphic-like disorder without repetitive behaviors: This is self-explanatory.
3. Body-focused repetitive behaviors (e.g., nail-biting, lip-biting, self-pinching, cheek-chewing), which have resulted in failed attempts to extinguish or reduce the behaviors.
4. Nondelusional obsessional jealousy, which involves a preoccupation with thoughts that one's partner is involved in infidelity. These beliefs may lead to the performance of repetitive behaviors (checking, calling, etc.) that cause clinically significant distress and disrupt the person's life.
5. *Koro:* An intense anxiety that the penis will recede into the body (in females the belief is about the vulva or nipples).
6. *Shubo-kyofu:* Intense fear of having a deformity (similar to body dysmorphic disorder).
7. *Jikoshu-kyofu* (olfactory reference syndrome): An intense fear of having a foul body odor.

Unspecified Obsessive-Compulsive and Related Disorder

This diagnosis is used in situations in which the symptoms do not meet all of the criteria of an obsessive-compulsive or related disorder, and the clinician does not have sufficient information to make a more specific diagnosis.

TRAUMA- AND STRESSOR-RELATED DISORDERS

As noted earlier, this new chapter in *DSM-5* combines childhood diagnosis of reactive attachment disorder with the adjustment disorders, acute stress disorder, PTSD, and others into one chapter focused on disorders in which a stressful or traumatic life event has precipitated the onset of symptoms. Exposure to stress or trauma can result in a wide range of symptoms, depending on age, previous exposure to trauma, temperament, and environmental factors. Internalizing symptoms (i.e., anxiety), externalizing symptoms (anger, aggression), or a mixture of both are possible. Following is a list of the heterogeneous disorders included in this chapter, along with their *ICD* codes.

ICD CODES AND *DSM* SPECIFIERS

TRAUMA- AND STRESSOR-RELATED DISORDERS

ICD-9-CM Code	Diagnosis	ICD-10-CM Code
313.89	Reactive Attachment Disorder	F94.1
313.89	Disinhibited Social Engagement Disorder	F94.2
309.81	Posttraumatic Stress Disorder	F43.10
308.3	Acute Stress Disorder	F43.0
Adjustment Disorders (code based on the following specifiers):		
309.0	Adjustment Disorder, with depressed mood	F43.21
309.24	Adjustment Disorder, with anxiety	F43.22
309.28	Adjustment Disorder, with mixed anxiety and depressed mood	F43.23
309.3	Adjustment Disorder, with disturbance of conduct	F43.24
309.4	Adjustment Disorder, with mixed disturbance of emotions and conduct	F43.25
309.9	Adjustment Disorder, unspecified	F43.20
309.89	Other Specified Trauma- and Stressor-Related Disorder	F43.8
309.9	Unspecified Trauma- and Stressor-Related Disorder	F43.9

We now turn to a discussion of each of the trauma- and stressor-related disorders with respect to any modifications from *DSM-IV*. The major change in *DSM-5* is the division of the two subtypes of reactive attachment disorder (inhibited versus disinhibited) into two distinct disorders that share the same etiology and prerequisite of social neglect (e.g., the absence of adequate caregiving). The neglect must occur before the age of 5 and limit the child's ability to form appropriate attachments. The distinction between the two disorders involves externalizing versus internalizing behavior and has implications across the lifespan.

Reactive Attachment Disorder (RAD)

The *DSM-5* criteria for RAD is the same as that in *DSM-IV-TR*, except, of course, the disinhibited subtype is no longer applied because it has become a distinct disorder. The child manifests symptoms of emotional withdrawal or inhibition toward caregivers, has limited positive affect, and rarely seeks or responds to comfort when distressed.

Disinhibited Social Engagement Disorder

The criteria for this new *DSM-5* disorder is similar to RAD in that the child must be at least 9 months old; the child has experienced social neglect or changes in caregivers to the point that appropriate attachments have not been formed; and the disorder is specified as persistent if it has been present for more than 12 months. In addition, to meet the criteria for this new disorder requires indiscriminate sociability with unfamiliar adults, manifested by at least two of the following:

- Reduced hesitancy in approaching and interacting with unfamiliar adults
- Being overly familiar with strangers (that is inconsistent with age-appropriate behavior or culture)
- Lack of concern about checking back with an adult caregiver, or wandering away without supervision
- Willingness to go off with an unfamiliar adult with little or no hesitation

Because social impulsivity is also a feature of ADHD, care should be taken to differentiate between the two disorders. Disinhibited social engagement disorder can also be comorbid with cognitive and language delays, stereotypies, and other conditions associated with neglect. However, symptoms of the disorder may persist long after the conditions of neglect have been eliminated, and children with this disorder may show no signs of disordered attachment (APA, 2013a).

Disinhibited social engagement disorder impairs a child's ability to interact in a culturally appropriate manner that is consistent with age-appropriate social boundaries. This may impact the child's relationships with adults and peers throughout their lifetime.

Assessment of attachment behavior should be part of a comprehensive biopsychosocial assessment. The development of this new disorder has implications for addressing the impact of relationships on the development, maintenance, and recovery of mental disorders. Prior to DSM-5, relational disorders were generally acknowledged as V codes (e.g., parent-child relational problem, upbringing away from parents, problems related to primary support group) and did not qualify for a diagnosis of a mental condition. Expanding attachment-related disorders into reactive attachment disorder and disinhibited social engagement disorder and applying the diagnostic criteria across the lifespan allows for consideration of the importance of relational processes on the development of mental disorders.

Before treatment can begin, serious neglect must first be assessed and environmental changes made to ensure adequate caregiving. Therapist characteristics and intervention strategies as outlined for RAD in *Selecting Effective Treatments* (Seligman & Reichenberg, 2012) are also appropriate for the treatment of this disorder, which may persist through adolescence. Future research will shed light on adolescent and adult manifestations of this disorder, which have not yet been determined.

Posttraumatic Stress Disorder

As mentioned earlier, significant changes have been made in the classification and conceptualization of PTSD, including reclassification as a trauma- and stressor-related disorder. Many of the diagnostic criteria remain the same as DSM-IV, but a significant number of alterations have been made. The criteria alone now fill nearly four pages of DSM-5 and include separate criteria for children 6 years and younger. Readers should refer to DSM-5 for a complete list of criteria for PTSD. Highlights of the changes between DSM-IV and DSM-5 include the following.

Criterion A is more explicit about what type of stressor qualifies as a traumatic event (e.g., sexual assault, actual or threatened death, serious injury) and requires discussion of whether the traumatic event(s) were experienced directly, witnessed, experienced indirectly, or the result of repeated exposure to details of traumatic events.

Criterion A2 from DSM-IV has been eliminated. As a result, it is no longer a requirement that a person must have intense fear, helplessness, or horror in reaction to the stressor.

The three symptom clusters in *DSM-IV* have been divided into four symptom clusters in *DSM-5*, with the addition of a behavioral symptom criterion:

1. Intrusion symptoms (e.g., intrusive memories, distressing dreams, dissociative reactions or flashbacks, intense distress, and physiological response to triggers)
2. Persistent avoidance of memories, thoughts, or feelings surrounding the traumatic event, or avoidance of external reminders (e.g., people, places)
3. Persistent negative alterations in cognitions and mood (e.g., numbing, cognitive distortions, detachment)
4. Hypervigilance or heightened arousal (e.g., aggression, angry outbursts, sleep disturbances, problems with concentration, reckless or self-destructive behavior)

In addition to revisions to clarify symptom expression, three new symptoms were added to the criteria listed previously:

- Persistent and distorted cognitions that lead the person to blame self or others
- Persistent negative emotional state (e.g., fear, horror, anger, guilt, shame)
- Reckless or self-destructive behavior

PTSD is now developmentally sensitive, in that diagnostic thresholds have been lowered for children older than age 6, and separate criteria are provided for children 6 years of age and younger. The major distinction with young children is that only one symptom of behavioral avoidance or negative alterations of cognition and mood is required. Longitudinal studies indicate that PTSD in childhood can persist into adulthood. Early-childhood trauma can create a biological vulnerability to other neurodevelopmental, learning, and externalizing disorders. Trauma experienced in mid-childhood or adolescence can lead to disorders of self-regulation, including eating disorders, substance use disorders, nonsuicidal self-injury, and criminal behavior. Early assessment and intervention, adapted to the child's developmental level, can reduce symptoms of PTSD in children.

DSM-5 includes the following specifiers for PTSD:

- With dissociative symptoms (e.g., depersonalization, or derealization)
- With delayed expression (in which full diagnostic criteria are not met until six months after the event)

The implications of these changes are legion. Assessment measures for PTSD are being revised to reflect changes in symptoms and criteria for diagnosis. Developmentally appropriate criteria are now available to diagnose childhood onset. This should result in earlier treatment and reduced pathology across the lifespan. More research is being conducted on pretraumatic factors (e.g., temperament, environment, and genetic and physiological factors) that lead to the development of PTSD. It is hoped that earlier detection and treatment will reduce the likelihood of developing one of the many comorbid disorders that people with PTSD are 80% more likely to acquire (e.g., substance use disorders; anxiety, depressive, and bipolar disorders; and oppositional defiant disorder and separation anxiety disorder in children).

Acute Stress Disorder

Changes in criteria for acute stress disorder are similar to those listed previously for PTSD (i.e., directly experiencing the traumatic event is no longer required, neither is an intense fear or horror as a reaction to the traumatic event; some symptoms have been clarified, and new symptoms have been added). Persons who report 9 out of 14 symptoms in the five categories of intrusion, negative mood, dissociation, avoidance, and arousal could be diagnosed with acute stress disorder. Symptoms must begin within 3 days and last up to a month for the diagnosis to be made. Symptoms that persist longer than 1 month, and meet the criteria for PTSD, would be diagnosed as PTSD.

Adjustment Disorders

Adjustment disorders are now considered to be trauma- and stressor-related disorders, and have been grouped with other disorders that occur after exposure to a significant life stressor (e.g., job loss, divorce). This placement provides greater clinical utility for the clinician in making a determination of the kinds of disorders to consider—all in one chapter.

The criteria for adjustment disorders remain the same as in *DSM-IV*. They are quite common, affecting as many as 5% to 20% of outpatients and nearly 50% of psychiatric inpatients. By definition, the stressor must have occurred within 3 months of symptom onset and resolve within 6 months of the stressor having ended. The subtypes (i.e., disturbances of mood, anxiety, or conduct) remain the same as in *DSM-5*. Many diagnoses of medical disorders are comorbid with adjustment disorders. Personality disorders, major depressive disorder, and PTSD should be ruled out. Cultural considerations should be taken into account, and clinicians should only make the diagnosis of adjustment disorder when the response to stress is greater than what would normally be expected.

Other Specified Trauma- and Stressor-Related Disorder

This category is used to diagnose other trauma- or stressor-related disorders that do not meet the criteria for one of the disorders in this section. The clinician then specifies the cause of the stressor (e.g., adjustment-like disorders with prolonged duration of more than 6 months without prolonged duration of stressor).

Unspecified Trauma- and Stressor-Related Disorder

This category includes subclinical diagnosis of a trauma- or stressor-related disorder in which the clinician chooses not to provide the reason why the criteria were not met and does not have enough information to make a specific diagnosis.

✳ ✳ ✳

DISSOCIATIVE DISORDERS

In *DSM-5* the chapter on dissociative disorders follows the chapter on trauma- and stressor-related disorders, indicating the closeness of the two classifications of disorders. Both PTSD and its precursor, acute stress disorder, can include depersonalization, derealization, amnesia, and other dissociative symptoms. A hallmark of dissociative disorders is the loss of continuity of experience, which can result in an inability to access information and fragmentation of identity. Several changes have been made in *DSM-5* that impact the diagnosis of disorders involving impairment in awareness of reality. The four distinct dissociative disorders found in

ICD CODES AND *DSM* SPECIFIERS

DISSOCIATIVE DISORDERS

ICD-9-CM Code	Diagnosis	ICD-10-CM Code
300.14	Dissociative Identity Disorder	F44.81
300.12	Dissociative Amnesia	F44.0
300.6	Depersonalization/Derealization Disorder	F48.1
300.15	Other Specified Dissociative Disorder	F44.89
300.15	Unspecified Dissociative Disorder	F44.9

DSM-IV have been merged into three disorders in *DSM-5*. (Dissociative fugue is no longer considered to be a condition but is listed as a specifier for dissociative amnesia.)

The overall prevalence rate for dissociative disorders is unknown. *DSM-5* reminds us that trance and possession phenomena are dissociative states that reflect commonly accepted ways of expressing distress in some cultures. Apart from the criteria changes listed as follows, the descriptions of dissociative disorders in *DSM-5* remain largely unchanged.

Dissociative Identity Disorder

Criterion A for dissociative identity disorder now specifies that transitions in identity may be observable by others as well as self-reported. Criterion A has also been expanded to include "certain possession-form phenomena and functional neurological symptoms to account for more diverse presentations of the disorder," although *DSM-5* considers the majority of possession states to be a normal part of spiritual practice and do not meet the criteria for DID. Criterion B allows for recurrent gaps in recall of everyday events and not just for traumatic experiences.

Dissociative Amnesia

The criteria for dissociative amnesia remains basically the same as in *DSM-IV*, with the exception that dissociative fugue—a condition in which identity amnesia is associated with travel or wandering—is now a specifier for dissociative amnesia in *DSM-5*.

Depersonalization/Derealization Disorder

The name of this disorder has been changed in *DSM-5* to incorporate derealization, which had been considered a symptom of depersonalization disorder in *DSM-IV*. Criterion A for depersonalization/derealization disorder now includes the presence of: depersonalization (experiences of unreality, or feeling detached from one's own thoughts or actions), derealization (experiences of unreality or detachment from one's surroundings), or both. The other criteria remain the same.

Because 95% of people who experience symptoms of this disorder do so prior to the age of 25, *DSM-5* recommends referral of patients over the age of 40 for underlying medical evaluation. Stress, immature defenses including denial of reality, projection, and idealization can contribute to this disorder, as can depression, anxiety, and illicit drug use, which must be ruled out.

Other Specified Dissociative Disorder and Unspecified Dissociative Disorder

Other specified dissociative disorders include: chronic syndromes of mixed dissociative symptoms; identity disturbances as a result of brainwashing, torture, or thought reform; acute dissociative reaction to stressful events (lasting less than 1 month); and dissociative trance (which is not associated with a cultural or religious practice). As in other unspecified disorders listed in *DSM-5*, unspecified dissociative disorder is diagnosed when the criteria for other specific dissociative disorders are not met, or the clinician does not have enough information to make a more specific diagnosis.

SOMATIC SYMPTOM AND RELATED DISORDERS

This new chapter in *DSM-5* identifies disorders characterized by thoughts, feelings, and behaviors related to somatic symptoms (previously referred to in *DSM-IV* as Somatoform Disorders). People who experience somatic symptoms frequently present in doctor's offices and other medical settings with symptoms that may result from medical disorders, may result from *concern* about a medical disorder, or may be factitious and inconsistent with any known medical or psychological disorder. Diagnosticians must use care, because neither the absence of a medical explanation nor the presence of a psychological problem automatically rules out the other.

One of the biggest changes in this section is the removal of unexplained symptoms as a key feature of somatic symptom disorders. For example, persons diagnosed under the new *DSM-5* guidelines with somatic symptom disorder may or may not have a diagnosed medical condition. The key feature of each somatic disorder is an excessive response—marked thoughts, feelings, and behaviors in excess of what would be expected—related to somatic symptoms. The new chapter on Somatic Symptom and Related Disorders is intended to provide clarification of the boundaries between disorders, minimize overlap between somatic disorders, and reduce the number of disorders and their subcategories.

For example, many of the somatoform disorders in *DSM-IV* have been reconceptualized in *DSM-5*. Pain disorder is now diagnosed as a specifier to Somatic Symptom Disorder (e.g., "with predominant pain"). Conversion disorder has been renamed Conversion Disorder (Functional Neurological Symptom Disorder), and hypochondriasis has been clarified, so that three-quarters of the people who met the criteria for hypochondriasis under *DSM-IV* would now be diagnosed with somatic symptom disorder in *DSM-5*. The other 25% who have high health-related anxiety but do not present with somatic symptoms would be diagnosed with illness anxiety disorder. More will be said about these changes later.

All of the disorders included in this new chapter share a preoccupation with somatic symptoms. Some may involve an unsubstantiated belief about a person's illness or the illness of another (as in factitious disorder), some may result from medically unexplained symptoms (as in functional neurological symptom disorder), and some may adversely affect an already known medical condition (such as anxiety aggravating asthma, or poor adherence to treatment). Each of the somatic symptom and related disorders is discussed in greater detail.

ICD CODE AND *DSM* SPECIFIERS

SOMATIC SYMPTOM AND RELATED DISORDERS

ICD-9-CM Code	Diagnosis	ICD-10-CM Code
300.82	Somatic Symptom Disorder	F45.1
300.7	Illness Anxiety Disorder	F45.21
300.11	Conversion Disorder (Functional Neurological Symptom Disorder) (*ICD-10* codes are based on specific symptoms; refer to *DSM-5*, pp. 318–319.)	
316	Psychological Factors Affecting Other Medical Conditions	F54
300.19	Factitious Disorder	F68.10
300.89	Other Specified Somatic Symptom and Related Disorder	F45.8
300.82	Unspecified Somatic Symptom and Related Disorder	F45.9

Somatic Symptom Disorder

Unlike *DSM-IV*'s somatization disorder, somatic symptom disorder in *DSM-5* does not require specific physical or sexual symptoms, occurrence before the age 30, or the presence of pain. Rather, somatic symptom disorder Criterion A requires a minimum of one somatic symptom that results in significant disruption of everyday life. Criterion B requires actions, thoughts, or feelings about the symptoms that are excessive in the amount of time devoted to them, out of proportion to the degree of seriousness, or include a high level of anxiety. Criterion C requires being symptomatic for a minimum of 6 months.

"With predominant pain" is now a specifier to somatic symptom disorder. This would have been diagnosed as pain disorder in *DSM-IV*. Other specifiers include "persistent" if symptoms have been of long duration, are particularly severe, or cause marked impairment. Severity levels (mild, moderate, and severe) should also be specified.

Illness Anxiety Disorder

As mentioned earlier, hypochondriasis has been reconceptualized. Anxiety and preoccupied thoughts of having or acquiring a serious illness must be present for a minimum of 6 months, with minimal or no somatic symptoms. If somatic symptoms are significant, the diagnosis of somatic symptom disorder would be more appropriate. *DSM-5* notes that nearly 75% of people who would have been diagnosed with hypochondriasis under *DSM-IV* will now be diagnosed with somatic symptom disorder. The other 25% will more appropriately be diagnosed with illness anxiety disorder.

Conversion Disorder (Functional Neurological Symptom Disorder)

People with this disorder may present with various types of unexplained neurological symptoms, including weakness, paralysis, tremors, or altered speech, hearing, or vision, among others. According to the new Criterion B for this disorder, clinical evidence must indicate that symptoms are incompatible with any known neurological or medical condition. Signs of inconsistency between medical exams, or exam results that are inconsistent when tested another way, would be sufficient. The overall clinical picture is important in making this diagnosis.

Symptom type specifiers have been added to help clarify functional neurological symptom disorder:

- Symptoms (e.g., with weakness or paralysis, with seizures, with mixed symptoms)
- Episode severity (acute or persistent)
- With or without psychological stressor (specify stressor, if appropriate)

Psychological Factors Affecting Other Medical Conditions (PFAMC)

Psychological factors, including stress, denial of symptoms, or anxiety, can adversely affect many medical conditions, including asthma, migraine, fibromyalgia, diabetes, and heart disease. This disorder has been repositioned in the Somatic Disorders chapter in *DSM-5*. It was previously listed in *DSM-IV* as an Other Condition That May Be a Focus of Clinical Attention. The prevalence rate of this disorder is unclear, but it may occur at any time across the lifespan.

The diagnostic criteria require the presence of a medical condition (other than a mental disorder) that affects the person in one of the following ways:

1. The psychological factors have affected the medical condition in an adverse way (e.g., delayed recovery).
2. The psychological factors interfere with treatment for a medical condition (e.g., poor adherence to treatment protocol).
3. The psychological factors create additional health risks.
4. The psychological factors influence or exacerbate the underlying medical problem and result in the need for medical attention.

The symptoms must not be better explained by another mental disorder, such as PTSD or panic disorder. Severity is specified by one of the following: mild (increases medical risk), moderate (aggravates underlying condition), severe (results in need for hospitalization), or extreme (severe, life-threatening risk).

Differential diagnosis requires distinguishing this disorder from psychological disorders that occur following diagnosis of a medical condition, which is more appropriately diagnosed as one of the adjustment disorders (as a response to an identifiable stressor). Somatic symptom disorder and illness anxiety disorder should also be ruled out.

Factitious Disorder

Factitious disorder has been moved to this chapter because somatic symptoms are predominant. Criteria that distinguished whether falsified symptoms were of medical or psychological origin have been removed from this disorder. Factitious Disorder by Proxy has been renamed Factitious Disorder Imposed on Another. Although rare, these disorders are most likely to be seen in medical settings, where they are estimated to affect about 1% of patients.

Other Specified Somatic Symptom and Related Disorder

This category includes symptoms that cause clinically significant distress but do not meet the criteria for any of the other somatic disorders. Specify if: brief somatic symptom disorder (of less than 6 months' duration); brief illness anxiety (less than 6 months); illness anxiety disorder without excessive health-related behaviors; or pseudocyesis (false belief of being pregnant).

Unspecified Somatic Symptom and Related Disorder

This category is reserved for presentations that do not meet the criteria for any of the somatic symptom and related disorders, and insufficient information is available for a more specified diagnosis.

FEEDING AND EATING DISORDERS

This new chapter in *DSM-5* incorporates several disorders that were first diagnosed in infancy, childhood, or adolescence, including pica and restrictive eating. The eating disorders (anorexia nervosa and bulimia nervosa) have been moved here, and binge-eating disorder (which was previously in the Appendix of *DSM-IV*) is now included as a distinct disorder. Finally, preliminary diagnostic criteria are included for other specified feeding and eating disorder and unspecified feeding or eating disorder. More information on each of these disorders is included as follows. All of the feeding and eating disorders are exclusive, with the exception of pica, which may be diagnosed in the presence of another feeding or eating disorder (APA, 2013a).

Pica and Rumination Disorder

Pica and rumination disorder are two distinct disorders from the *DSM-IV* chapter on disorders that are usually first diagnosed in childhood. Although

ICD CODES AND DSM SPECIFIERS

FEEDING AND EATING DISORDERS

ICD-9-CM Code	Diagnosis	ICD-10-CM Code
307.52	Pica—Children	F98.3
	Pica—Adults	F50.8
307.53	Rumination Disorder	F98.21
307.59	Avoidant/Restrictive Food Intake Disorder	F50.8
307.1	Anorexia Nervosa, specify either:	
	Restricting type	F50.01
	Binge-eating/purging type	F50.02
307.51	Bulimia Nervosa	F50.2
307.51	Binge-Eating Disorder	F50.8
307.59	Other Specified Feeding or Eating Disorder	F50.8
307.50	Unspecified Feeding or Eating Disorder	F50.9

they have been moved to the chapter on Feeding and Eating Disorders in *DSM-5*, the diagnostic criteria for these disorders remain basically the same as in *DSM-IV*.

Avoidant/Restrictive Food Intake Disorder (Formerly Feeding Disorder of Infancy or Early Childhood)

The criteria have been significantly expanded for this disorder. Food avoidance, restricted nutritional intake, or lack of interest in eating is most common in infancy or early childhood and may persist throughout adulthood. This disorder can be diagnosed at any age for those who meet Criterion A, and if the condition is not better explained by: the presence of an eating disorder, another medical condition, a co-occurring mental disorder, a culturally sanctioned practice (e.g., religious fasting), or a lack of available food.

For Criterion A to be met, patients must have an eating disturbance that causes them to fail to consume adequate nutrition for their energy needs. and they must exhibit one or more of the following:

- Has lost a significant amount of weight or failure to gain age-appropriate weight if an infant or child.
- Notable nutrition deficiency.
- Oral supplements or enteral feeding have become necessary to maintain adequate nutritional intake (e.g., children with failure to thrive, adults who require tube feeding in the absence of a medical condition).
- The condition causes significant interference with psychosocial functioning.

In some situations, food avoidance or restriction may be the result of heightened sensitivity to smells, texture, or taste. Food avoidance may also occur after an unpleasant experience (e.g., vomiting or choking on food). Developmentally normal restriction of food, as in toddlers who are picky eaters or elderly adults who have reduced food intake, would not meet the criteria for this disorder, unless it is clinically significant as previously described in criterion A. The disorders that co-occur most frequently with avoidant/restrictive food intake disorder are neurodevelopmental disorders (such as autism spectrum, ADHD, and intellectual disability), anxiety, and OCD.

Anorexia Nervosa

The core diagnostic criteria for anorexia nervosa is the same as in *DSM-IV*, except for the following three changes:

1. The amenorrhea criterion has been eliminated.
2. The diagnostic threshold has been lowered, which reduces the large number of people who had been diagnosed with Eating Disorder NOS.
3. The following new severity specifiers have been developed for adults, based on the Body Mass Index (BMI).
   - Mild: BMI greater than or equal to $17 \ kg/m^2$
   - Moderate: BMI $16–16.99 \ kg/m^2$
   - Severe: BMI $15–15.99 \ kg/m^2$
   - Extreme: BMI less than $15 \ kg/m^2$

   Note: The CDC BMI percentile calculator is used for children and adolescents.

Bulimia Nervosa

Bulimia nervosa, in which recurrent episodes of binge eating are accompanied by inappropriate compensatory behaviors (purging, misuse of laxatives or diuretics, excessive exercise) has also undergone some revisions from *DSM-IV*. The core criteria in *DSM-5* lowers the diagnostic threshold for bulimia nervosa and now requires that bingeing or compensatory purging behaviors occur at least once per week for a 3-month period. The purging/nonpurging subtype specifier has been eliminated from *DSM-5*. In partial or full remission can now be specified. Severity specifiers for bulimia nervosa are based on the average number of inappropriate compensatory behaviors per week, and may be increased to reflect the degree of funtional disability or other symptoms of the disorder. Specify:

- Mild: 1 to 3 episodes of inappropriate compensatory behaviors weekly
- Moderate: 4 to 7 episodes
- Severe: 8 to 13 episodes
- Extreme: 14 or more episodes

All eating disorders are physically damaging and potentially life threatening, so a complete assessment should include a referral for a physical exam, as well as obtaining a history of the client's dieting and weight loss across the lifespan. Any compensatory activities (e.g., laxative abuse, purging) should also be monitored.

Binge-Eating Disorder (BED)

Binge eating is now a full-fledged disorder in *DSM-5*, and its diagnostic criteria remain largely the same as listed in the Appendix of *DSM-IV*, except the criteria has been changed to require an average of one episode weekly over a 3 month period. In other words, binge-eating disorder is described as recurrently eating in a distinct period of time an amount of food that is substantially larger than most people would consume in the same situation; accompanied by feeling out of control, or as if one could not stop eating. Episodes of binge eating include at least three of the following:

- Eating large amounts even when not hungry
- Embarrassment over the amount of food that is eaten and therefore eating alone

- Eating much faster than usual
- Eating until physically uncomfortable
- Experiencing feelings of guilt or disgust after the episode of overeating

To qualify as binge-eating disorder, the episodes must occur at least once a week for 3 months and be accompanied by negative affect, guilt, shame, disgust, or other feelings of distress. Binge eating is not accompanied by the use of compensatory behaviors such as overexercise, purging, or fasting, and is not better accounted for by a diagnosis of anorexia nervosa or bulimia nervosa.

Readers should note that although binge-eating disorder is frequently associated with obesity, most persons with obesity do not binge-eat, and therefore do not meet the criteria for this disorder. Conversely, it is also possible for a person of normal weight, or one who is overweight but not obese, to meet the full criteria for binge-eating disorder.

Unlike anorexia and bulimia, which are more common among White females who are either middle or upper SES, BED occurs across all races, nationalities, socioeconomic levels, and has a higher representation of men. Increased body mass index (BMI) is associated with increased medical problems and use of health care facilities. Men, who make up 40% of those diagnosed with BED, can be particularly vulnerable to the health risks associated with this disorder and are 3 times more likely to develop metabolic syndrome. Obesity itself is not a psychiatric disorder, but can be comorbid with many *DSM-5* disorders including BED, depression, and increased suicide risk.

When diagnosing binge-eating disorder, the following course specifiers should be noted:

- In full or partial remission
- Severity level, ranging from mild (1 to 3 binge-eating episodes), moderate (4 to 7 episodes), severe (8 to 13 episodes), to extreme (14 or more episodes) per week

Treatment for binge-eating disorder is similar to treatment for bulimia nervosa, specifically CBT, DBT, interpersonal therapy (IPT), and mindfulness-based cognitive therapy. To date, CBT and IPT exhibit the most empirical support in randomized controlled trails (Alexander, Goldschmidt, & Le Grange, 2013). CBT, as part of a culturally competent intervention, helps persons to change their thoughts about physical appearance and body image and has been shown to have a success rate as high as 50% for BED while also reducing comorbidity of other *DSM-5* disorders, particularly depression. But DBT, self-help programs, and training in mindfulness have also shown promise. Because many people with BED have experienced trauma or physical abuse in childhood, treatment using eye movement desensitization and reprocessing may also be appropriate.

Other Specified Feeding or Eating Disorder (Formerly Eating Disorder NOS)

This category is appropriate for use in the following five situations:

1. The client does not meet the full criteria for bulimia nervosa.
2. The client does not meet the full criteria for binge-eating disorder.
3. The behavior is solely a purging disorder in the absence of overeating.
4. The criteria for anorexia are met, but the client's weight remains within the normal range (atypical anorexia).
5. As a diagnosis of night-eating syndrome, in which the person has recurrent episodes of eating at night, eating after awakening from sleep, or consuming large amounts of food after the regular dinnertime.

Unspecified Feeding or Eating Disorder

This category can be used when symptoms of an eating disorder are present and severe enough to cause distress or impairment in one or more areas of functioning, but the criteria for a specific feeding or eating disorder are not met, or not enough information is available to make a more definitive diagnosis.

ELIMINATION DISORDERS

As mentioned earlier, encopresis and enuresis have been moved to a new chapter on Elimination Disorders. No significant changes have been made to the criteria for these disorders in *DSM-5*. For a complete discussion of the criteria, assessment, and treatment interventions for elimination disorders, refer to Seligman and Reichenberg (2012).

ICD CODES AND *DSM* SPECIFIERS

ELIMINATION DISORDERS

ICD-9-CM Code	Diagnosis	*ICD-10-CM* Code
307.6	Enuresis	F98.0
307.7	Encopresis	F98.1
Other Specified Elimination Disorder		
788.39	With urinary symptoms	N39.498
787.60	With fecal symptoms	R15.9
Unspecified Elimination Disorder		
788.30	With urinary symptoms	R32
787.60	With fecal symptoms	R15.9

* * *

SLEEP-WAKE DISORDERS

In *DSM-5*, a new chapter has been created specifically for Sleep-Wake Disorders, which contains the same primary subgroups of sleep disorders as *DSM-IV*, as listed here.

ICD CODES AND *DSM* SPECIFIERS

SLEEP-WAKE DISORDERS

ICD-9-CM Code	Diagnosis	*ICD-10-CM* Code
307.42	Insomnia Disorder	F51.01
307.44	Hypersomnolence Disorder	F51.11
__.__	Narcolepsy	__.__
347.00	Narcolepsy without cataplexy	G47.410
347.01	Narcolepsy with cataplexy	G47.411

ICD-9-CM Code	Diagnosis	ICD-10-CM Code
Breathing-Related Sleep Disorders		
Breathing-related sleep disorders, such as sleep apnea, sleep-related hypoventilation, and circadian rhythm sleep-wake disorders, must be determined by polysomnography and coded based on cause. (Refer to *DSM-5*, pp. 378–398, for specific details.)		
Parasomnias		
__.__	Non–Rapid Eye Movement Sleep Arousal Disorders	__.__
307.46	Sleepwalking type	F51.3
307.46	Sleep terror type	F51.4
307.47	Nightmare Disorder	F51.5
327.42	Rapid Eye Movement Sleep Behavior Disorder	G47.52
333.94	Restless Legs Syndrome	G25.81
__.__	Substance/Medication-Induced Sleep Disorder	__.__
Coding Note: See substance-specific codes and *ICD-9-CM* and *ICD-10-CM* coding. Specify if: With onset during intoxication, With onset during withdrawal Specify whether: insomnia type, daytime sleepiness type, parasomnia type, mixed type		
780.52	Other Specified Insomnia Disorder	G47.09
780.52	Unspecified Insomnia Disorder	G47.00
780.54	Other Specified Hypersomnolence Disorder	G47.19
780.54	Unspecified Hypersomnolence Disorder	G47.10
780.59	Other Specified Sleep-Wake Disorder	G47.8
780.59	Unspecified Sleep-Wake Disorder	G47.9

Parasomnias

It bears noting that the field of sleep disorders has grown exponentially since the publication of *DSM-IV*, and biological validators for diagnosis are now used in *DSM-5*. Scientific studies, including polysomnography, are often helpful in determining diagnosis for many of the sleep-wake disorders, including narcolepsy, restless legs syndrome, and breathing-related sleep disorders.

Although sleep disorders related to another mental disorder and sleep disorders due to a general medical condition have been removed from *DSM-5*, many sections have been expanded to reflect the current level of knowledge now available on the subject. For example, breathing-related sleep disorders have been divided into three distinct disorders: obstructive sleep apnea, central sleep apnea, and sleep-related hypoventilation. Rapid eye movement sleep behavior disorder and restless legs syndrome (formerly Sleep Disorders NOS) have become independent disorders. Also, pediatric and developmental criteria are now integrated into the text where appropriate.

SEXUAL DYSFUNCTIONS

The following disorders constitute the new *DSM-5* chapter on Sexual Dysfunctions.

ICD CODES AND DSM SPECIFIERS

SEXUAL DYSFUNCTIONS

ICD-9-CM Code	Diagnosis	ICD-10-CM Code
302.74	Delayed Ejaculation	F52.32
302.72	Erectile Disorder	F52.21
302.73	Female Orgasmic Disorder	F52.31
302.72	Female Sexual Interest/Arousal Disorder	F52.22
302.76	Genito-Pelvic Pain/Penetration Disorder	F52.6
302.71	Male Hypoactive Sexual Desire Disorder	F52.0
302.75	Premature (Early) Ejaculation	F52.4
291.89	Substance/Medication-Induced Sexual Dysfunction, Alcohol*	
292.89	Substance/Medication-Induced Sexual Dysfunction, Other Substances*	
302.79	Other Specified Sexual Dysfunction	F52.8
302.70	Unspecified Sexual Dysfunction	F52.9

*ICD-10-CM codes are based on degree of severity and the presence of a use disorder. Refer to *DSM-5*, pp. 446–447, for additional details.

The majority of the changes to the *DSM-5* chapter on sexual dysfunctions include the following:

- The female sexual desire and arousal disorders were combined into one disorder (female sexual interest/arousal disorder).
- Sexual aversion disorder was removed, due to a lack of supporting research.
- All sexual dysfunctions now require a minimum duration of 6 months or more, with the exception of substance/medication-induced sexual dysfunction.
- More precise criteria are set for degree of severity.
- All sexual dysfunctions can be divided into two subtypes: (1) lifelong versus acquired, and (2) generalized versus situational. *Lifelong* refers to problems that have been present since the first sexual experience, and *acquired* relates to disorders that occur after a relatively healthy period of sexual experience. *Generalized* subtype refers to sexual problems that are not related to specific experiences, situations, or partners; *situational* subtype refers to those problems that only occur in conjunction with specific contexts.
- Genito-pelvic pain/penetration disorder has been added as a new disorder that combines vaginismus and dyspareunia, which were previously comorbid disorders that were difficult to distinguish under *DSM-IV*.

DSM-5 also includes information on associated factors that may correlate with sexual dysfunctions, including medical factors, partner factors, relationship factors, individual vulnerability factors, and cultural or religious factors. If severe relationship distress or other stressors seem a more appropriate explanation of the symptoms of sexual difficulties, then the appropriate V or Z code for the relationship problem or stressor should be used instead of the sexual dysfunction.

GENDER DYSPHORIA (FORMERLY GENDER IDENTITY DISORDER)

Gender Identity Disorder (GID), as defined in *DSM-IV-TR*, was a controversial diagnosis, and the term was considered to be pejorative by people whose gender at birth was contrary to the gender they later identified with. *DSM-5* has changed important criteria and renamed the disorder Gender Dysphoria. The following specific disorders are included in this new *DSM-5* chapter.

ICD CODES AND DSM SPECIFIERS

GENDER DYSPHORIA

ICD-9-CM Code	Diagnosis	ICD-10-CM Code
302.6	Gender Dysphoria in Children	F64.2
302.85	Gender Dysphoria in Adolescents and Adults	F64.1
302.6	Other Specified Gender Dysphoria	F64.8
302.6	Unspecified Gender Dysphoria	F64.9

As with all other disorders listed in *DSM-5*, a critical element of determining the presence of a disorder is the presence of clinically significant distress associated with the condition. In other words, doubts about one's gender or gender nonconformity do not constitute a mental disorder. Rather, clinically significant distress or impairment in social, occupational, or other important areas of functioning must be present (APA, 2013a). *DSM-5* contains separate sets of criteria for children, adolescents, and adults, and reconceptualizes the phenomenon as gender incongruence rather than identification with the gender other than the one a person was born with.

Specific criteria for gender dysphoria include:

- A marked difference exists between the person's expressed gender and the gender others would assign to him or her.
- These feelings must be present for at least 6 months.
- In children, the desire to be another gender must be present and verbalized.
- Clinically significant distress or impairment in social, occupational, or other important areas of functioning must be experienced.

A new specifier has been added to identify clients who have undergone medical treatment in support of the new gender assignment.

Readers are reminded that gender identity is a fluid concept that encompasses feelings about the body, social roles, gender identification, and sexuality. The therapist's comfort level and attitudes can affect the client's disclosure of sexual topics. Treatment can be complicated, especially if clients are considering gender reassignment surgery. Therapists who are not comfortable or who lack experience working with this population should refer clients to a qualified therapist who has experience working with gender dysphoria.

DISRUPTIVE, IMPULSE-CONTROL, AND CONDUCT DISORDERS

Lack of emotional and behavioral self-control are the hallmark of the behaviors in this new chapter in *DSM-5*. The two disruptive behavior disorders of childhood (Oppositional Defiant Disorder and Conduct Disorder) have been subsumed into this new chapter. Following is a complete list of the disorders in this chapter, along with their *ICD* codes.

ICD CODES AND *DSM* SPECIFIERS

DISRUPTIVE, IMPULSE-CONTROL, AND CONDUCT DISORDERS

ICD-9-CM Code	Diagnosis	ICD-10-CM Code
313.81	Oppositional Defiant Disorder Specify current severity: mild, moderate, severe	F91.3
312.34	Intermittent Explosive Disorder	F63.81
Conduct Disorder		
312.81	Childhood-Onset Type	F91.1
312.82	Adolescent-Onset Type	F91.2
312.89	Unspecified Onset Specify if with limited prosocial emotions Specify current level of severity (mild, moderate, severe)	F91.9
301.7	Antisocial Personality Disorder	F60.2
312.33	Pyromania	F63.1
312.32	Kleptomania	F63.2
312.89	Other Specified Disruptive, Impulse-Control, and Conduct Disorder	F91.8
312.9	Unspecified Disruptive, Impulse-Control, and Conduct Disorder	F91.9

Because it is thought to be on a continuum with ODD and conduct disorder, antisocial personality disorder is included both here and in the chapter on Personality Disorders. For the most part, the criteria for these disorders remain the same except for the following changes.

Oppositional Defiant Disorder

High levels of emotional reactivity and frustration intolerance form the basis of this disorder, which often results in frequent conflicts with parents, teachers, supervisors, and other people. Oppositional defiant disorder is characterized by three types of symptoms:

1. Angry/irritable mood
2. Argumentative/defiant behavior
3. Vindictiveness (being spiteful at least twice in the most recent 6-month period)

The criteria are the same as in *DSM-IV* and the behavior must include at least four symptoms and be observable for at least 6 months. The severity of symptoms, as measured by the persistence and frequency of these behaviors and their presence in one (mild), two (moderate), or three (severe) settings, should be used to distinguish the disorder from behavior that is considered age-appropriate. For children younger than 5, the behavior should occur on most days for a period of at least 6 months. Individual temperament (e.g., poor frustration tolerance, high emotional reactivity); inconsistent, harsh, or neglectful parenting; and a number of genetic factors have been associated with the development of oppositional defiant disorder.

Intermittent Explosive Disorder

Impulsive aggressive outbursts disproportionate to the provocation or psychosocial stressor are the core feature of this disorder. Physical aggression is no longer a requirement of intermittent explosive disorder. Nondestructive and noninjurious physical aggression and verbal aggression are now sufficient to diagnose this condition, which also includes a minimum age of 6 (or equivalent developmental level) for diagnosis. Enhanced criteria delineate the frequency and nature of the outbursts, which must include four or more symptoms in the past 6 months, and include either three incidents of physical assault or destruction of property in a 1-year period or verbal aggression (i.e., impulsive and/or anger based). As with all disorders, symptoms must cause personal distress, difficulties in relationships or employment, or result in legal or financial problems. The impulsive, rather than premeditated, nature of the outbursts distinguishes IED from conduct disorder.

Conduct Disorder

Exclusionary criteria for conduct disorder have been removed from *DSM-5*, and a new specifier "with limited prosocial emotions" has been added. This has also been referred to as the "callous and unemotional" specifier, in the literature, and is only indicated if the person meets two or more of the following characteristics in multiple relationships and settings over a minimum of a 12-month period:

- Lack of remorse or guilt—is not remorseful or concerned about the person being hurt.
- Callous—lack of empathy: unconcerned about the feelings of others; concerned only about the effects on himself or herself; cold or uncaring about others.
- Unconcerned about performance—lacks concern about school or work performance, does not put forth effort, blames others for poor performance.
- Shallow or deficient affect—does not express feelings or emotions to others except in shallow, self-serving ways (e.g., manipulative emotions, emotions that contradict behavior).

Age of onset for conduct disorder can be specified as childhood-onset (before the age of 10), adolescent-onset (after the age of 10), or unspecified onset (age of onset unknown). This specifier is diagnostically significant in terms of the future course of the disorder, with those with childhood onset having a more guarded prognosis and requiring more multisystemic treatment approaches.

Level of severity is specified as:

- Mild—few conduct problems in excess of those needed to diagnose
- Moderate—neither mild nor severe
- Severe—many symptoms in excess of the number required to diagnose, or severe harm has been caused to others (e.g., rape, use of a weapon, physical cruelty)

According to *DSM-5*, the context in which conduct disorders occur should be considered (e.g., war zones, high-crime areas). Gender also plays a role, with males tending to exert both physical and relational aggression, whereas females tend to exhibit more relational aggression and lying. In general, impulsive and oppositional behavior tends to increase during the preschool years and adolescence. Care must be taken to ensure that the frequency and intensity of the symptoms are beyond what is normative for the child's age and stage of development.

ADHD is commonly comorbid with all of the disruptive, impulse-control, and conduct disorders, and its co-occurrence is associated with more severe outcomes. It would seem that ADHD belongs in this chapter, as it is conceptualized as being on a continuum with ODD, conduct disorder, and antisocial personality disorder. However, because of the large body of research supporting the neurological underpinnings of ADHD, it is located in the neurodevelopmental chapter of *DSM-5*.

Pyromania

The diagnostic criteria for this rare disorder, which is estimated to affect less than 1% of the population, remain the same as those listed in *DSM-IV*.

Kleptomania

This disorder is also rare, affecting 0.3% to 0.6% of the population. Females constitute 75% of the people who meet the criteria for kleptomania. No changes have been made to the *DSM-IV* criteria for kleptomania. A complete discussion of diagnosis, assessment, and treatment for this disorder can be found in *Selecting Effective Treatments* (Seligman & Reichenberg, 2012).

Other Specified Disruptive, Impulse-Control, and Conduct Disorder

This diagnosis is given in situations in which the clinician can specify why the criteria for a specific disorder were not met. For example, the outbursts do not meet the frequency level required.

Unspecified Disruptive, Impulse-Control, and Conduct Disorder

This is the preferred diagnosis when the clinician does not wish to specify the reason why criteria are not met, or, as in the case of an emergency room presentation, adequate information is not available to make a specific diagnosis.

* * *

SUBSTANCE-RELATED AND ADDICTIVE DISORDERS

Major changes have been made to the *DSM-5* section on alcohol and other substance-related disorders. The most significant changes include: (1) merging the two distinct disorders of substance abuse and substance dependence into one disorder: substance use disorder; (2) requiring two criteria to be met for this disorder (*DSM-IV* required only one criterion for the diagnosis of abuse); (3) adding cannabis withdrawal and caffeine withdrawal as new disorders; and (4) reclassifying gambling disorder as the first behavioral disorder to be included in this new Substance-Related and Addictive Disorders section of *DSM-5*. Following is a list of each disorder (preceded by the appropriate code from *ICD-9-CM* and followed by the *ICD-10-CM* code). Additional changes are discussed in further detail next.

ICD CODES AND *DSM* SPECIFIERS

SUBSTANCE-RELATED AND ADDICTIVE DISORDERS

ICD-9-CM Code	Diagnosis	ICD-10-CM Code
Alcohol-Related Disorders		
__.__	Alcohol Use Disorder (specify current level of severity)	__.__
305.00	Mild	F10.10
303.90	Moderate	F10.20
303.90	Severe	F10.20
303.00	Alcohol Intoxication (specify current level of severity)	__.__
	With use disorder, mild	F10.129
	With use disorder, moderate or severe	F10.229
	Without use disorder	F10.929
291.81	Alcohol Withdrawal	__.__
	Without disturbances of perception	F10.239
	With disturbances of perception	F10.232
__.__	Other Alcohol-Related Disorders	__.__
291.9	Unspecified Alcohol-Related Disorder	__.__

(continued)

(continued)

ICD-9-CM Code	Diagnosis	ICD-10-CM Code
Caffeine-Related Disorders		
305.90	Caffeine Intoxication	F15.929
292.0	Caffeine Withdrawal	F15.93
—.—	Other Caffeine-Induced Disorders (Note: Caffeine-induced anxiety and caffeine-induced sleep disorders have been moved to chapters on anxiety and sleep-related disorders.)	—.—
292.9	Unspecified Caffeine-Related Disorder	F15.99
Cannabis-Related Disorders		
—.—	Cannabis Use Disorder (specify current level of severity)	—.—
305.20	Mild	F12.10
304.30	Moderate	F12.20
304.30	Severe	F12.20
292.89	Cannabis Intoxication (*ICD-10* codes require specifiers; see *DSM-5*, p. xxvi.)	—.—
292.0	Cannabis Withdrawal	F12.288
—.—	Other Cannabis-Related Disorders	—.—
292.9	Unspecified Cannabis-Related Disorder	F12.99
Hallucinogen-Related Disorders		
—.—	Phencyclidine Use Disorder (specify current level of severity)	—.—
305.90	Mild	F16.10
304.60	Moderate	F16.20
304.60	Severe	F16.20
—.—	Other Hallucinogen Use Disorder (specify current level of severity)	—.—
305.30	Mild	F16.10
304.50	Moderate	F16.20
304.50	Severe	F16.20

ICD-9-CM Code	Diagnosis	ICD-10-CM Code
292.89	Phencyclidine Intoxication	
	With use disorder, mild	F16.129
	With use disorder, moderate or severe	F16.229
	Without use disorder	F16.929
292.89	Other Hallucinogen Intoxication	
	With use disorder, mild	F16.129
	With use disorder, moderate or severe	F16.229
	Without use disorder	F16.929
292.89	Hallucinogen Persisting Perception Disorder	F16.983
__.__	Other Phencyclidine-Induced Disorders	__.__
__.__	Other Hallucinogen-Induced Disorders	__.__
292.9	Unspecified Phencyclidine-Related Disorder	F16.99
292.9	Unspecified Hallucinogen-Related Disorder	F16.99

Inhalant-Related Disorders

ICD-9-CM Code	Diagnosis	ICD-10-CM Code
__.__	Inhalant Use Disorder (specify current level of severity)	__.__
305.90	Mild	F18.10
304.60	Moderate	F18.20
304.60	Severe	F18.20
292.89	Inhalant Intoxication (specify current level of severity)	__.__
	With use disorder, mild	F18.129
	With use disorder, moderate or severe	F18.229
	Without use disorder	F18.929
__.__	Other Inhalant-Induced Disorders	__.__
292.9	Unspecified Inhalant-Related Disorder	F18.99

Opioid-Related Disorders

ICD-9-CM Code	Diagnosis	ICD-10-CM Code
__.__	Opioid Use Disorder (specify current level of severity)	__.__
305.50	Mild	F11.10
304.00	Moderate	F11.20
304.00	Severe	F11.20

(continued)

(continued)

ICD-9-CM Code	Diagnosis	ICD-10-CM Code
292.89	Opioid Intoxication (specify current level of severity) (*IDC-10* codes require specifiers; see *DSM-5*, p. xxvii.)	__.__
292.0	Opioid Withdrawal	F11.23
__.__	Other Opioid-Induced Disorders	__.__
292.9	Unspecified Opioid-Related Disorder	F11.99

Sedative-, Hypnotic-, or Anxiolytic-Related Disorders

ICD-9-CM Code	Diagnosis	ICD-10-CM Code
__.__	Sedative-, Hypnotic-, or Anxiolytic Use Disorder (specify current level of severity)	__.__
305.40	Mild	F13.10
304.10	Moderate	F13.20
304.10	Severe	F13.20
292.89	Sedative-, Hypnotic-, or Anxiolytic Intoxication (specify current level of severity)	__.__
	With use disorder, mild	F13.129
	With use disorder, moderate or severe	F13.229
	Without use disorder	F13.929
292.0	Sedative-, Hypnotic-, or Anxiolytic Withdrawal	
	Without disturbances of perception	F13.239
	With disturbances of perception	F13.232
__.__	Other Sedative-, Hypnotic-, or Anxiolytic-Induced Disorders	__.__
292.9	Unspecified Sedative-, Hypnotic-, or Anxiolytic-Related Disorder	F13.99

Stimulant-Related Disorders

ICD-9-CM Code	Diagnosis	ICD-10-CM Code
	(See *DSM-5*, p. xxviii, for specific codes for cocaine, amphetamine, and other stimulant use disorders.)	
__.__	Stimulant Use Disorder (specify current level of severity)	__.__

ICD-9-CM Code	Diagnosis	ICD-10-CM Code
__.__	Mild	__.__
305.70	Amphetamine-type substance	F15.10
305.60	Cocaine	F14.10
305.70	Other or unspecified stimulant	F15.10
__.__	Moderate	__.__
304.40	Amphetamine-type substance	F15.20
304.20	Cocaine	F14.20
304.40	Other or unspecified stimulant	F15.20
__.__	Severe	__.__
304.40	Amphetamine-type substance	F15.20
304.20	Cocaine	F14.20
304.40	Other or unspecified stimulant	F15.20
	Stimulant Intoxication (Specify the specific intoxicant)	__.__
292.89	Amphetamine or other stimulant, Without perceptual disturbances	__.__
	With use disorder, mild	F15.129
	With use disorder, moderate or severe	F15. 229
	Without use disorder	F15.929
292.89	Cocaine, Without perceptual disturbances	__.__
	With use disorder, mild	F14.129
	With use disorder, moderate or severe	F14.229
	Without use disorder	F14.929
292.89	Amphetamine or other stimulant, with perceptual disturbances	__.__
	With use disorder, mild	F15.122
	With use disorder, moderate or severe	F15.122
	Without use disorder	F15.922
292.0	Stimulant Withdrawal	__.__
	Specify the specific substance causing withdrawal	__.__
	Amphetamine or other stimulant	F15.23
	Cocaine	F14.23

(continued)

(continued)

ICD-9-CM Code	Diagnosis	ICD-10-CM Code
292.9	Unspecified Stimulant-Related Disorders	__.__
	Amphetamine or other stimulant	F15.99
	Cocaine	F14.99
Tobacco-Related Disorders		
__.__	Tobacco Use Disorder (specify current level of severity)	__.__
305.1	Mild	Z72.0
305.1	Moderate	F17.200
305.1	Severe	F17.200
292.0	Tobacco Withdrawal	F17.203
__.__	Other Tobacco-Induced Disorders	__.__
292.9	Unspecified Tobacco-Related Disorder	F17.209
Other (or Unknown) Substance-Related Disorders		
__.__	Other (or Unknown) Substance Use Disorder (specify current level of severity)	__.__
305.90	Mild	F19.10
304.90	Moderate	F19.20
304.90	Severe	F19.20
292.89	Other (or Unknown) Substance Intoxication (specify current level of severity)	__.__
	With use disorder, mild	F19.129
	With use disorder, moderate or severe	F19.229
	Without use disorder	F19.929
292.0	Other (or Unknown) Substance Withdrawal	F19.239
__.__	Other (or Unknown) Substance-Induced Disorders	__.__
292.9	Unspecified Other (or Unknown) Substance-Related Disorder	F19.99
Non-Substance-Related Disorders		
312.31	Gambling Disorder (Specify if episodic or persistent. Also specify current level of severity: mild, moderate, severe)	F63.0

DSM-5 combines the categories of substance abuse and substance dependence into one all-encompassing disorder: substance use disorder. The change results from research indicating that abuse and dependence are not distinct disorders but part of a continuum. In a further change, two criteria are now necessary for diagnosis (*DSM-IV* required the endorsement of only one criterion). This eliminates the "diagnostic orphan" problem of *DSM-IV*.

Critics of the new *DSM-5* approach to substance abuse note that eliminating the one-criterion diagnosis, which was available in *DSM-IV*, will result in a large number of people who really do have problematic drinking not being diagnosed. The new changes in *DSM-5* are also inconsistent with the World Health Organization's *ICD-10* criteria.

Members of the Substance Use Disorder Work Group for *DSM-5* report that reviews of data on more than 100,000 cases diagnosed using the two different criteria sets (in *DSM-IV* and *DSM-5*) resulted in little change in the number diagnosed (Schuckit, 2012). The rationale for the change is to make diagnosis easier for the clinician, because it no longer requires the maintenance of two separate sets of criteria (O'Brien, 2012; Schuckit, 2012). By default, this should also make the diagnosis easier to understand for the person being diagnosed.

The new diagnosis of substance use disorder adopts the spectrum approach, with degree of severity being qualified as "mild," "moderate," and "severe."

The clinical implications of these and other changes to this section of *DSM-5* include the following:

- Clinicians will have one disorder to treat, which will reduce confusion and eliminate the need to distinguish between two criteria sets—one for abuse and a separate set for dependence.
- The new requirement that two symptoms instead of one must be endorsed for diagnosis recognizes that substance use disorders are a pattern of behavior, rather than just one problem area.
- Diagnostic criteria have been combined and strengthened into a list of 11 symptoms.
- A craving criterion (or a strong desire or urge to use the substance) has been added to *DSM-5*, bringing it closer into alignment with *ICD-9*, published by the World Health Organization.
- The diagnosis of polysubstance dependence has been removed. When more than one substance use disorder is diagnosed, each should be recorded individually.
- Severity of the substance use disorder is now based on the number of symptoms that are met. For example, if the client endorses two or

three symptoms, then the diagnosis is "mild substance use disorder"; four or five symptoms is considered "moderate"; and six or more is "severe."

- The previous symptom of substance-related legal problems has been dropped from DSM-5. Although arrests for driving under the influence (DUI) are a major reason why people seek treatment for substance use disorders, it was not found to be predictive of dysfunction or indicative of level of severity. Also removed is the specifier "with or without physiological dependence."
- New specifiers have been added for "in a controlled environment" and "on maintenance therapy" as the case may be.
- "Early remission" from a substance use disorder is defined in DSM-5 as having 3 to 12 months elapse without meeting any criteria (except craving) for the disorder. "Sustained remission" is specified if 12 months or more have passed without meeting any criteria except craving or a strong desire or urge to use the substance.

The following 10 separate classes of drugs considered in DSM-IV-TR remain the same in DSM-5:

1. Alcohol
2. Caffeine
3. Cannabis
4. Hallucinogens
5. Inhalants
6. Opioids
7. Sedatives, Hypnotics, and Anxiolytics
8. Stimulants
9. Tobacco
10. Other (or unknown) substances

A distinction is made between substance use disorders and substance-induced disorders. Substance-induced disorders are:

- Intoxication
- Withdrawal
- Other substance/medication-induced mental disorders (e.g., substance-induced psychosis, substance-induced depressive disorder)

DSM-5 provides an overview of this information as well as recording and coding procedures for each disorder. Readers who work with clients with substance use disorders should carefully read the relevant substance-related disorder section in DSM-5 for diagnostic criteria, course specifiers, and recording procedures. For example, Criterion A of alcohol use disorder specifies a pattern of use leading to impairment or distress, with the new requirement of at least 2 of the following 11 symptoms being met in a 12-month period:

1. Drinks more than intended, or for longer than intended
2. Efforts to control or cut back on drinking have been unsuccessful
3. Large amounts of time are spent obtaining, using, or recovering from alcohol
4. Cravings (the presence of a strong desire to drink)
5. Recurrent use resulting in problems at work, home, or school
6. Continued use despite recurrent social or interpersonal problems resulting from drinking
7. Curtailing important activities in favor of alcohol use
8. Alcohol use despite potentially hazardous outcomes (drinking and driving, for example)
9. Continued alcohol use despite knowledge that alcohol use is causing or exacerbating a persistent physical or psychological problem
10. Tolerance or a need for increased amounts of alcohol
11. Withdrawal symptoms

If the person indicates the presence of two or more symptoms, an alcohol use disorder would be diagnosed. Coding is based on the current level of severity:

- Mild: presence of two to three symptoms
- Moderate: presence of four to five symptoms
- Severe: presence of six or more symptoms

If there have been no symptoms in the past 3 months or longer, two remission specifiers can be considered: "in early remission" (3 to 12 months of not meeting the criteria for alcohol use disorder) or "in sustained remission" (12 months or longer without meeting any of the criteria). An exception is the presence of "craving or a strong desire to use alcohol," which may still be experienced even while in early or sustained remission.

Specify if remission is "in a controlled environment," to indicate if the person has restricted access to alcohol (e.g., locked hospital unit, jail, therapeutic communities). For example, a person with years of recurrent alcohol use who meets more than six of the criteria and has been incarcerated for the past year might be coded as follows:

303.90 Alcohol Use Disorder, Severe, In sustained remission, in a controlled environment

Caffeine Withdrawal

Also new to *DSM-5*, caffeine withdrawal has been added as a viable disorder with four sets of criteria including: prolonged daily use, abruptly stopping caffeine use followed within 24 hours by at least three of the following symptoms: headache, fatigue, bad mood or irritability, lack of concentration, and flu-like symptoms. These symptoms cause significant distress and are not better accounted for by another medical condition or mental disorder.

Cannabis Withdrawal

Unlike cannabis use and cannabis intoxication, which were listed in *DSM-IV*, cannabis withdrawal is new to *DSM-5*. Cannabis withdrawal occurs after a heavy or prolonged period in which cannabis was used most days for several months. Symptoms occur within 7 days and must include three or more of the symptoms of irritability, anxiety, difficulty sleeping, reduced appetite, depressed mood, restlessness, and at least one physical symptom (e.g., headache, sweating). *DSM-5* includes a coding note that cannabis withdrawal can only occur in conjunction with a moderate or severe cannabis use disorder.

Gambling Disorder

Only one non-substance-related disorder, gambling, is included in the Substance-Related and Addictive Disorders chapter of *DSM-5*, although the criteria remain the same as in *DSM-IV*. The rationale for moving a behavioral disorder to this section of *DSM-5* includes scientific evidence that indicates gambling activates areas of the brain similar to the brain's reward systems that are activated by substances. Other repetitive behaviors that could lead people to have difficulties if they are not controlled (such as shopping, gaming, and sex) do not have sufficient peer-reviewed research to be labeled as mental disorders at this time. Of these three, Internet Gaming Disorder is the only one that is included in *DSM-5*'s Section III: Conditions for Further Study. By moving gambling disorder into the Substance-Related and Addictive Disorders chapter of *DSM-5*, the implication can be made that additional behavioral syndromes will be recognized as mental disorders at a future date.

Some professionals have heralded the *DSM-5* changes in substance use disorder as "a good start," while also wishing that the APA had included quantitative data based on the correlation between frequency and quantity of substance use and increased risk of disease and death (Lembke, Bradley, Henderson,

Moos, & Harris, 2011). Such information is currently available, although lacking in *DSM-5*, which Lembke (2013) notes may be due, in part, to the difficulty of quantifying substances such as marijuana, heroin, or prescription drugs into standard units. It is much easier to quantify standard units of alcohol.

Although the information is not necessary for determining a *DSM-5* diagnosis, clinicians should continue to assess quantity of use and motivation to change, so they can prepare appropriate treatment plans, recognizing that clients with substance use disorders may deny, obscure, or underreport their symptoms. A tendency to minimize or normalize substance-related problems is inherent in substance use disorders. Clinicians must address any ambivalence or lack of motivation to change early on in the assessment process, if treatment is to be successful with this population.

NEUROCOGNITIVE DISORDERS

The neurocognitive disorders category includes a group of disorders in which a deficit in cognitive function that is acquired rather than developmental is the primary clinical manifestation. Delirium, dementia, amnestic, and other cognitive disorders have been moved in *DSM-5* to the chapter on Neurocognitive Disorders. Major Neurocognitive Disorder involves significant decline in one or more cognitive domains (e.g., executive function) from a previous level of functioning. Dementia has been subsumed under major neurocognitive disorder, although it can also be listed as a symptom in the subtypes where it is frequently found to occur.

Mild neurocognitive disorder is a new disorder in *DSM-5* that permits the identification of less severe symptoms of cognitive impairment. It is intended to distinguish between mild and severe cognitive impairment, with the intention of providing earlier treatment for a slower progression of the neurocognitive disorder. For example, if a modest decline in cognitive functioning is apparent, but does not interfere with independent living, a mild neurocognitive disorder might be diagnosed.

The criteria for Neurocognitive Disorders are based on defined cognitive domains (e.g., executive function, learning and memory, complex attention, language, perceptual and motor skills). A detailed discussion of cognitive domain symptoms and assessments for major and mild neurocognitive disorders is provided in *DSM-5* Table 1 (APA, 2003a, pp. 593–595). Although cognitive deficits may also be present in other mental disorders including schizophrenia, only disorders whose main features are cognitive are considered in the Neurocognitive Disorders category. These disorders are not present at

ICD CODES AND *DSM* SPECIFIERS

NEUROCOGNITIVE DISORDERS

Delirium

Major or Mild Neurocognitive Disorders

Unspecified Neurocognitive Disorder

Coding Note: *ICD-9-CM* and *ICD-10-CM* coding for Delirium, Major and Mild Neurocognitive Disorders, and Unspecified Neurocognitive Disorder is very complex and will not be repeated here. Each neurocognitive disorder may be substance- or medication-induced, may be due to another medical condition, may have multiple etiologies, or may be specified or unspecified. To determine the appropriate code, most of the neurocognitive disorders must first be determined to be major or mild, with or without disturbances of behavior, and the level of severity (mild, moderate, or severe) must be specified. Readers who are interested in coding for the Neurocognitive Disorders section should consult pages 591–641 of *DSM-5* or refer to the appropriate edition of WHO's ICD codes.

birth, and when they occur, they represent a decline from previous levels of functioning. Unlike any of the other disorders included in the *DSM-5*, diagnosis of the pathology and often the etiology of neurocognitive disorders can frequently be determined.

More substantive changes to the Neurocognitive Disorders chapter include a distinction among the following specifiers:

- Due to Alzheimer's disease
- Frontotemporal degeneration
- With Lewy bodies
- Vascular neurocognitive disorder
- Due to traumatic brain injury
- Substance/medication-induced
- Due to HIV infection
- Due to Prion disease
- Due to Parkinson's disease
- Due to Huntington's disease
- Due to another medical condition
- Due to multiple etiologies

Clients presenting with symptoms of dementia or other cognitive impairments should first be referred to a physician for a complete medical and neurological assessment. Therapists working with this population usually work closely with the medical community to develop assessment and treatment plans. For a complete look at assessments, symptoms, severity factors, and coding for the Neurocognitive Disorders, refer to pages 591–643 in *DSM-5*.

PERSONALITY DISORDERS

Despite many years of research and an exploration of a radical revision to the diagnosis of personality disorders, in the end the APA's Board of Trustees voted not to implement structural change to the personality disorders section at this time. However, an alternative *DSM-5* Model for Personality Disorders is included in *DSM-5*'s Section III: Emerging Methods and Models for additional study and research. At the present time, the personality disorders and their codes remain the same as in *DSM-IV*.

ICD CODES AND *DSM* SPECIFIERS

PERSONALITY DISORDERS

ICD-9-CM Code	Diagnosis	ICD-10-CM Code
301.0	Paranoid Personality Disorder	F60.0
301.20	Schizoid Personality Disorder	F60.1
301.22	Schizotypal Personality Disorder	F21
301.7	Antisocial Personality Disorder	F60.2
301.83	Borderline Personality Disorder	F60.3
301.50	Histrionic Personality Disorder	F60.4
301.81	Narcissistic Personality Disorder	F60.81
301.82	Avoidant Personality Disorder	F60.6
301.6	Dependent Personality Disorder	F60.7
301.4	Obsessive-Compulsive Personality Disorder	F60.5
310.1	Personality Change Due to Another Medical Condition	F07.0
301.89	Other Specified Personality Disorder	F60.89
301.9	Unspecified Personality Disorder	F60.9

PARAPHILIC DISORDERS

A paraphilia is an intense and persistent interest in sexual arousal and gratifica-
tion based on fantasizing and engaging in sexual behavior involving objects
(e.g., fetishism, scatologia, or obscene telephone calls), suffering or humilia-
tion (e.g., masochism, sadism), or children or nonconsenting partners (e.g.,
pedophilia, exhibitionism). In *DSM-IV*, a paraphilia was considered to be a
disorder. In *DSM-5*, the wording has been changed so that only a paraphilia
that is currently causing distress or impairment to the individual or a paraphilia
whose satisfaction has entailed personal harm, or risk of harm, to others rises to
the level of a disorder. Thus, a paraphilia is a necessary prerequisite to having a
paraphilic disorder, but a paraphilia is not a disorder in and of itself.

In other words, only the more severe paraphilic disorder meets the criteria
for a mental disorder.

The paraphilic disorders retain the same criteria, assessment, and treatment interventions as the paraphilias in *DSM-IV*. Only the name has been
changed from paraphilia to Paraphilic Disorder to underscore that while
having a paraphilia is necessary for the diagnosis of paraphilic disorder, it is
not enough to warrant diagnosis of a mental disorder. The paraphilia must
also cause distress or impairment to the individual, or the fulfillment of the
paraphilia must involve personal harm, or risk of harm, to others in order to
meet the criteria of a paraphilic disorder (APA, 2013a).

ICD CODES AND *DSM* SPECIFIERS

PARAPHILIC DISORDERS

ICD-9-CM Code	Diagnosis	ICD-10-CM Code
302.82	Voyeuristic Disorder	F65.3
302.4	Exhibitionistic Disorder	F65.2
302.89	Frotteuristic Disorder	F65.81
302.83	Sexual Masochism Disorder	F65.51
302.84	Sexual Sadism Disorder	F65.52
302.2	Pedophilic Disorder	F65.4
302.81	Fetishistic Disorder	F65.0
302.3	Transvestic Disorder	F65.1
302.89	Other Specified Paraphilic Disorder	F65.89
302.9	Unspecified Paraphilic Disorder	F65.9

To make a diagnosis of Paraphilic Disorder, persons must satisfy both Criterion A and Criterion B. Criterion A provides the qualitative measures of the specific disorder. Criterion B requires the presence of distress and impairment (e.g., depression, employment problems, difficulty in social relationships) or that the person has acted on these sexual urges with a nonconsenting person. Those who satisfy Criterion A but not B would be said to have a paraphilia, but not a paraphilic disorder.

The following course specifiers have been added to the diagnostic criteria for all paraphilic disorders:

- In full remission, which is defined as: "The individual has not acted on the urges with a nonconsenting person, and there has been no distress or impairment in social, occupational, or other areas of functioning, for at least 5 years while in an uncontrolled environment." (APA, 2013a, p. 687)
- In a controlled environment (specifically living in an institution or other setting in which the behavior is restricted)

Clinician-rated and self-rated measures and severity assessments can be helpful in determining the diagnosis. "Other specified paraphilic disorder" can be diagnosed in cases in which symptoms do not meet the full criteria for a paraphilic disorder, or if the symptoms of recurrent and intense sexual arousal occur in relation to other behaviors not delineated in the *DSM-5*. Although only eight paraphilias are listed in *DSM-5*, dozens have been identified (e.g., zoophilia, scatologia, necrophilia), and almost any of the paraphilias could rise to the level of a paraphilic disorder as a result of negative consequences for the individual or others. "Unspecified paraphilic disorder" is used in situations in which the clinician chooses not to specify the reason that the criteria have not been met for a specific paraphilic disorder, including situations in which there is insufficient information.

An example of coding for a person with a paraphilic disorder involving animals and who is currently incarcerated might be:

302.89 [F65.89] Other specified paraphilic disorder, zoophilia, in a controlled environment

OTHER MENTAL DISORDERS

Four disorders are included in this section that apply to presentations that cause symptoms characteristic of mental disorders and cause clinically significant distress but do not meet the full criteria for any other mental disorder

ICD CODES AND DSM SPECIFIERS

OTHER MENTAL DISORDERS

ICD-9-CM Code	Diagnosis	ICD-10-CM Code
294.8	Other Specified Mental Disorder Due to Another Medical Condition	F06.8
294.9	Unspecified Mental Disorder Due to Another Medical Condition	F09
300.0	Other Specified Mental Disorder	F99
300.9	Unspecified Mental Disorder	F99

in *DSM-5*. Before giving a diagnosis of other specified mental disorder due to another medical condition, clinicians must first determine that the symptoms are caused by the physiological effects of another medical condition. If so, the medical condition should be coded and recorded first. For example, dissociative symptoms due to complex partial seizures would be coded and recorded as:

345.40 [G40.209] complex partial seizures
294.8 [F06.8] other specified mental disorder due to complex partial seizures, dissociative symptoms

MEDICATION-INDUCED MOVEMENT DISORDERS AND OTHER ADVERSE EFFECTS OF MEDICATION

Some medications prescribed for the treatment of mental disorders have the untoward side effect of causing movement disorders (e.g., muscular rigidity, tremor). Other medications, such as antidepressants, can cause symptoms when they are discontinued. Although these disorders are not mental disorders, they are included in *DSM-5* because medication is used in the treatment of mental disorders and other conditions. Most cases of medication-induced movement disorders occur in the first month of treatment and remit after medication has been discontinued. Although rare, the development of neuroleptic malignant syndrome is a possibility in any person being treated with antipsychotic medication.

ICD CODES AND *DSM* SPECIFIERS

MEDICATION-INDUCED MOVEMENT DISORDERS AND OTHER ADVERSE EFFECTS OF MEDICATION

ICD-9-CM Code	Diagnosis	ICD-10-CM Code
332.1	Neuroleptic-Induced Parkinsonism	G21.11
332.1	Other Medication-Induced Parkinsonism	G21.19
333.92	Neuroleptic Malignant Syndrome	G21.0
333.72	Medication-Induced Acute Dystonia	G24.02
333.99	Medication-Induced Acute Akathisia	G25.71
333.85	Tardive Dyskinesia	G24.01
333.72	Tardive Dystonia	G24.09
333.99	Tardive Akathisia	G25.71
333.1	Medication-Induced Postural Tremor	G25.1
333.99	Other Medication-Induced Movement Disorder	G25.79
__.__	Antidepressant Discontinuation Syndrome	__.__
995.29	Initial encounter	T43.205A
995.29	Subsequent encounter	T43.205D
995.29	Sequelae	T43.205S
__.__	Other Adverse Effect of Medication	__.__
995.20	Initial encounter	T50.905A
995.20	Subsequent encounter	T50.905D
995.20	Sequelae	T50.905S

OTHER CONDITIONS THAT MAY BE A FOCUS OF CLINICAL ATTENTION

Other conditions that may affect the diagnosis and treatment of mental disorders are also included in *DSM-5*. Although these conditions are not mental disorders, they may contribute to the current visit or might help explain the need for additional testing or treatment. These other conditions (referred to as "V-codes" in *DSM-IV*), which may otherwise impact the patient's care, vary widely and may include relational problems, psychological or sexual abuse, violence, problems with housing, education, or economic problems, religious or spiritual problems, problems related to crime or other legal problems, and problems related to health care, such as unavailability of treatment, nonadherence to treatment, malingering, and others.

Although these conditions are not mental disorders, they provide a background and help clinicians understand some of the underlying circumstances the person may be facing that may impact treatment now and into the future. These codes should be listed along with the mental health diagnosis, even though they might not be the cause of the current office visit.

Following is a select list of conditions from *ICD-9* (usually V-codes) and *ICD-10* (usually Z-codes). The World Health Organization's complete

ICD CODES AND *DSM* SPECIFIERS

OTHER CONDITIONS THAT MAY BE A FOCUS OF CLINICAL ATTENTION

ICD-9-CM Code	Other Conditions	ICD-10-CM Code
Relational Problems		
V61.20	Parent-Child Relational Problem	Z62.820
V61.8	Sibling Relational Problem	Z62.891
V61.8	Upbringing Away from Parents	Z62.29
V61.29	Relationship Distress with Spouse or Intimate Partner	Z63.0
V61.03	Disruption of Family by Separation or Divorce	Z63.5
V61.8	High Expressed Emotion Level Within Family	Z63.8
V62.82	Uncomplicated Bereavement (i.e., normal grieving as reaction to the death of a loved one)	Z63.4
Maltreatment, Abuse and Neglect		

Coding Note: Codes for conditions of abuse and neglect are determined based on the following specifiers:
  Whether child or adult victim
  Initial or subsequent encounters
  Confirmed or suspected abuse
  Physical or sexual abuse

ICD-9-CM Code	Other Conditions	ICD-10-CM Code
	Whether the perpetrator or the victim Other circumstances including past history of abuse, mental health services, etc. Whether spouse, partner, or other person	
Educational Problems		
V62.3	Academic or Educational Problem	Z55.9
Occupational Problems		
V62.21	Problem Related to Current Military Deployment Status	Z56.82
V62.29	Other Problem Related to Employment	Z56.9
Housing Problems		
V60.0	Homelessness	Z59.0
V60.1	Inadequate Housing	Z59.1
V60.89	Discord with Neighbor, Lodger, or Landlord	Z59.2
V60.6	Problem Related to Living in an Institution	Z59.3
Economic Problems		
V60.2	Lack of Adequate Food or Safe Drinking Water	Z59.4
V60.2	Extreme Poverty	Z59.5
V60.2	Low Income	Z59.6
V60.2	Insufficient Social Insurance or Welfare Support	Z59.7
Other Problems		
V62.89	Phase of Life Problem	Z60.0
V62.4	Acculturation Difficulty	Z60.3
V62.4	Target of (Perceived) Adverse Discrimination or Persecution	Z60.5

(continued)

(continued)

ICD-9-CM Code	Other Conditions	ICD-10-CM Code
Problems Related to Crime/Legal System		
V62.89	Victim of Crime	Z65.4
V62.5	Imprisonment or Other Incarceration	Z65.1
V62.5	Problems Related to Release From Prison	Z65.2
V62.5	Problems Related to Other Legal Issues	Z65.3
Other Problems Related to Counseling, Psychosocial, and Environment		
V65.49	Sex Counseling	Z70.9
V65.40	Other Counseling or Consultation (religious, nutrition, etc.)	Z71.9
V62.89	Religious or Spiritual Problem	Z65.8
V61.7	Problems Related to Unwanted Pregnancy	Z64.0
V62.89	Victim of Terrorism or Torture	Z65.4
V62.22	Exposure to Disaster, War, or Other Hostility	Z65.5
V62.89	Other Problem Related to Psychosocial Circumstances	Z65.8
Other Circumstances or Personal History		
V15.49	Other Personal History of Psychological Trauma	Z91.49
V15.59	Personal History of Self-Harm	Z91.5
V62.22	Personal History of Military Deployment	Z91.82
V15.89	Other Personal Risk Factors	Z91.89
V60.3	Problems Related to Living Alone	Z60.2
V69.9	Problem Related to Lifestyle (poor sleep hygiene, lack of physical exercise, high risk behaviour)	Z72.9
V71.01	Adult Antisocial Behavior (not due to a mental disorder, e.g., organized crime, drug dealers)	Z72.811

ICD-9-CM Code	Other Conditions	ICD-10-CM Code
V71.02	Child or Adolescent Antisocial Behavior	Z72.810
V15.81	Nonadherence to Medical Treatment	Z91.19
278.00	Overweight or Obesity	E66.9
V65.2	Malingering	Z76.5
V40.31	Wandering Associated with a Mental Disorder (mental disorder must first be coded)	Z91.83
V62.89	Borderline Intellectual Functioning	R41.83

list of conditions and *ICD-10* codes can be found online at www.who.int/classifications/icd/en. Thirteen pages of conditions and codes are also included in the *DSM-5* (beginning on page 715).

Suspected or confirmed child maltreatment or neglect (physical abuse, sexual abuse, neglect, psychological abuse) can be an important factor in the assessment and treatment of mental disorders. A prior history of any of these life circumstances or environmental stressors should be coded along with the disorder as useful information that is relevant to the person's care, even if it is not the cause of the current office visit.

Chapter 3

EMERGING MEASURES AND MODELS

D SM-5's Section III provides assessment measures that can help facilitate diagnosis of the conditions listed in Section II, along with cultural
formulation interviews, an alternative model for personality disorders, and
criteria sets for conditions that require further study. Each of these areas is
discussed briefly here.

ASSESSMENT MEASURES

In support of DSM-5's dimensional approach to diagnosis discussed earlier
in this book, the following list of assessment measures, accompanied by
scoring and interpretation guidelines, are available from the American Psychiatric Association and the World Health Organization. A limited number
of dimensional and cross-cutting assessments are published in the print edition of DSM-5. A larger number of assessments were made available after
the DSM-5 was published and are available for download free of charge at
www.psychiatry.org/practice/dsm/dsm5/online-assessment-measures
   Specific measures and their availability are listed below:

- *Level 1 Cross-Cutting Measures*
  DSM-5 includes two cross-cutting questionnaires that help clinicians
  determine other potential areas of concern that could impact the client's
  diagnosis. Using a 5-point Likert scale ranging from None or not at all
  (0) to Severe (nearly every day), adults are asked to endorse 13 symptom
  domains (e.g., depression, anger, repetitive thoughts) and children
  and adolescents are assessed on 12 domains (e.g., somatic symptoms,

inattention, irritability). The goal is to identify additional areas that may have an impact on the person's assessment, treatment, and prognosis. The results of these symptom measures can also be used to track changes in symptoms over time and document any improvement and progress.

The following two cross-cutting symptom measures are available in the print version of *DSM-5*—one is a self-rated assessment of symptoms for adults, and the other is for children between the ages of 6 and 17, which is intended to be completed by parents or guardians.

1. Self-Rated Level 1 Cross-Cutting Symptom Measure—Adult (available in print version, *DSM-5*, p. 738)
2. Parent/Guardian-Rated DSM-5 Level 1 Cross-Cutting Symptom Measure—Child Age 6–17 (see *DSM-5*, p. 740)

- *Level 2 Cross-Cutting Symptom Measures* (available for download online) Sometimes the results of Level 1 assessments indicate more in-depth (Level 2) symptom measures are needed. Level 2 cross-cutting measures are available for most of the symptom domains covered in Level 1. Online versions are available for download for the following Level 2 Measures:

For Adults
LEVEL 2—Depression—Adult (PROMIS Emotional Distress—Depression—Short Form)

LEVEL 2—Anger—Adult (PROMIS Emotional Distress—Anger—Short Form)

LEVEL 2—Mania—Adult (Altman Self-Rating Mania Scale [ASRM])

LEVEL 2—Anxiety—Adult (PROMIS Emotional Distress—Anxiety—Short Form)

LEVEL 2—Somatic Symptom—Adult (Patient Health Questionnaire 15 Somatic Symptom Severity Scale [PHQ-15])

LEVEL 2—Sleep Disturbance—Adult (PROMIS—Sleep Disturbance—Short Form)

LEVEL 2—Repetitive Thoughts and Behaviors—Adult (Adapted from the Florida Obsessive-Compulsive Inventory [FOCI] Severity Scale [Part B])

LEVEL 2—Substance Use—Adult (Adapted from the NIDA-Modified ASSIST)

For Parents of Children Ages 6–17
LEVEL 2—Somatic Symptom—Parent/Guardian of Child Age 6–17 (Patient Health Questionnaire 15 Somatic Symptom Severity Scale [PHQ-15])

LEVEL 2—Sleep Disturbance—Parent/Guardian of Child Age 6–17 (PROMIS—Sleep Disturbance—Short Form)

LEVEL 2—Inattention—Parent/Guardian of Child Age 6–17 (Swanson, Nolan, and Pelham, version IV [SNAP-IV])

LEVEL 2—Depression—Parent/Guardian of Child Age 6–17 (PROMIS Emotional Distress—Depression—Parent Item Bank)

LEVEL 2—Anger—Parent/Guardian of Child Age 6–17 (PROMIS Emotional Distress—Calibrated Anger Measure—Parent)

LEVEL 2—Irritability—Parent/Guardian of Child Age 6–17 (Affective Reactivity Index [ARI])

LEVEL 2—Mania—Parent/Guardian of Child Age 6–17 (Adapted from the Altman Self-Rating Mania Scale [ASRM])

LEVEL 2—Anxiety—Parent/Guardian of Child Age 6–17 (Adapted from PROMIS Emotional Distress—Anxiety—Parent Item Bank)

LEVEL 2—Substance Use—Parent/Guardian of Child Age 6–17 (Adapted from the NIDA-Modified ASSIST)

For Children Ages 11–17

LEVEL 2—Somatic Symptom—Child Age 11–17 (Patient Health Questionnaire 15 Somatic Symptom Severity Scale [PHQ-15])

LEVEL 2—Sleep Disturbance—Child Age 11–17 (PROMIS—Sleep Disturbance—Short Form)

LEVEL 2—Depression—Child Age 11–17 (PROMIS Emotional Distress—Depression—Pediatric Item Bank)

LEVEL 2—Anger—Child Age 11–17 (PROMIS Emotional Distress—Calibrated Anger Measure—Pediatric)

LEVEL 2—Irritability—Child Age 11–17 (Affective Reactivity Index [ARI])

LEVEL 2—Mania—Child Age 11–17 (Altman Self-Rating Mania Scale [ASRM])

LEVEL 2—Anxiety—Child Age 11–17 (PROMIS Emotional Distress—Anxiety—Pediatric Item Bank)

LEVEL 2—Repetitive Thoughts and Behaviors—Child Age 11–17 (Adapted from the Children's Florida Obsessive Compulsive Inventory [C-FOCI] Severity Scale)

LEVEL 2—Substance Use—Child Age 11–17 (Adapted from the NIDA-Modified ASSIST)

- *Disorder-Specific Severity Measures for Adults*
  Clinician-Rated Dimensions of Psychosis Symptom Severity (available in print version, p. 743)

  Severity Measure for Depression—Adult (Patient Health Questionnaire [PHQ-9])

  Severity Measure for Separation Anxiety Disorder—Adult

  Severity Measure for Specific Phobia—Adult

  Severity Measure for Social Anxiety Disorder (Social Phobia)—Adult

  Severity Measure for Panic Disorder—Adult

  Severity Measure for Agoraphobia—Adult

  Severity Measure for Generalized Anxiety Disorder—Adult

  Severity of Posttraumatic Stress Symptoms—Adult (National Stressful Events Survey PTSD Short Scale [NSESS])

  Severity of Acute Stress Symptoms—Adult (National Stressful Events Survey Acute Stress Disorder Short Scale

- *World Health Organization Disability Assessment Schedule 2.0*
  A hand-scored simple version of the World Health Organization Disability Assessment Schedule (WHODAS 2.0) is included in *DSM-5* (see pages 745–748). WHODAS 2.0 provides a useful assessment scale that may also be used to track treatment progress at regular intervals. The APA recommends that clinicians link in to the eHRS (electronic health record system) for more complex assessments of symptoms (APA, 2013a, p. 745).

CULTURAL FORMULATION

A Cultural Formulation section is included in *DSM-5* to help clinicians recognize and consider the richness of cultural concepts, rules, and practices in the lives of their clients. Cultural formulation interviews can help increase awareness of how cultural context can influence presentation of mental illness and subsequently influence diagnosis. *DSM-5* expands on the Outline for Cultural Formulation that was included in *DSM-IV*, and provides a suggested Cultural Formulation Interview (CFI) with suggestions for follow-up questions. An informant version (CFI-Informant) is also included and can be used to supplement information obtained by the CFI or, if the individual is unable to provide information (e.g., due to cognitive dysfunction or florid psychosis), may actually replace the CFI.

An outline for cultural formulation, based on *DSM-IV* material, provides a framework for assessing and understanding cultural features of a client's mental health problem. The outline calls for assessment of the client in the following areas:

- Cultural identity
- Cultural conceptualizations of distress
- Psychosocial stressors and cultural features of vulnerability and resilience
- Cultural features of the clinical relationship between client and clinician
- Overall cultural assessment

The Cultural Formulation Interview is a set of 16 questions that can be used by clinicians to conduct a culturally competent mental health assessment. Two types of interviews are included in the print version of *DSM-5*:

1. Cultural Formulation Interview (CFI) (*DSM-5*, pp. 752–754)
2. Cultural Formulation Interview (CFI)—Informant Version (*DSM-5*, pp. 755–757)

When additional information would be beneficial, Supplementary Modules to the Cultural Formulation Interview are available online to help clinicians conduct a more comprehensive cultural assessment. The first eight supplementary modules provide follow-up questions to explore the following domains of the core CFI in greater depth:

1. Explanatory Module
2. Level of Functioning
3. Social Network
4. Psychosocial Stressors
5. Spirituality, Religious, and Moral Issues
6. Cultural Identification
7. Coping and Help-Seeking
8. Patient-Client Relationship

The next three modules focus on populations with specific needs, such as children and adolescents, older adults, and immigrants and refugees. The last module explores the experiences and views of individuals who perform caregiving functions.

Other tools are included in the print version of *DSM-5* to assist clinicians expand their cultural competency in relation to mental health assessment, including:

- *Glossary of cultural concepts of distress.* Many concepts of distress specific to a particular culture may share similarities with psychiatric disorders (e.g., mood, anxiety, somatic symptoms), but may be normative expressions of acute distress within that culture (e.g., "attack of nerves" in Latin culture). Presentations of such symptoms may or may not meet the full criteria for diagnosis. To help clinicians understand concepts of distress within a cultural context, DSM-5 includes a Glossary of Cultural Concepts of Distress on pages 833–837.

- *Data in criteria and text for specific disorders.* Culture-related diagnostic issues are included in DSM-5, where appropriate, for each of the diagnostic categories. Clinicians should refer to the specific disorder for additional culture-related information.
- *Enhanced V codes and Z codes.* Culturally relevant V codes and Z codes (e.g., acculturation problems, religious or spiritual problems) are included in the DSM-5 section on Other Conditions That May Be a Focus of Clinical Attention (see pages 715–727).

ALTERNATIVE MODEL FOR DIAGNOSING PERSONALITY DISORDERS

The alternative DSM-5 model for diagnosing personality disorders is intended to be easier and more intuitive for clinicians to use. The alternative model of personality disorders retains the most useful aspects of the categorical system and also retains six personality disorders: antisocial, avoidant, borderline, narcissistic, obsessive-compulsive, and schizotypal. Another category called personality disorder—trait specified (PD-TS) was created for persons who meet the general criteria for a personality disorder but who do not have one of the previously specified disorders. PD-TS would replace the PD-NOS category from DSM-IV-TR.

The 20-page description of the new methodology is too extensive to be included here. Clinicians who would like to explore how the alternative model could enhance their diagnosis of personality disorders, or learn how it can be used to assess personality functioning and traits in the absence of a personality disorder, can find the full version of the alternative model on pages 761–781 of DSM-5.

Section III also includes material on disorders that are proposed for future research, similar to the appendix material in DSM-IV-TR. It is these disorders for further study that we turn to next.

CONDITIONS FOR FURTHER STUDY

The inclusion in DSM-5 of eight conditions for further study is based on extensive research. The following criteria sets, although not found to have sufficient evidence to warrant their inclusion as official diagnoses at this time, are no exception. Accordingly, the specific items, thresholds, and durations for each of the conditions for further study were determined by consensus of the experts, based on literature review, data reanalysis, and field trial results (APA, 2013a, p. 783).

Some disorders (e.g., Binge Eating Disorder) have been moved from the Appendix of *DSM-IV-TR* into Section III based on the preponderance of research. Similarly, categories and conditions that appeared in the Appendix to *DSM-IV* have been removed after additional research failed to produce enough evidence to warrant their inclusion as individual disorders.

The following conditions for further study are not intended for clinical use, but rather to encourage future research. It is important to note, however, that if at any point clinically significant manifestations of these proposed disorders are exhibited, they should be coded as "Other Specified." The eight proposed disorders in *DSM-5* include:

1. Attenuated psychosis syndrome
2. Depressive episodes with short-duration hypomania
3. Persistent complex bereavement disorder
4. Caffeine use disorder
5. Internet gaming disorder
6. Neurobehavioral disorder due to prenatal alcohol exposure (ND-PAE)
7. Nonsuicidal self-injury (NSSI)
8. Suicidal behavior disorder

Attenuated Psychosis Syndrome

Magical thinking, perceptual distortions, and difficulty with frontal lobe functions (e.g., lack of concentration, disorganization, cognitive dysfunction) are hallmarks of attenuated psychosis. Based on current studies, only one-third of people with a first diagnosis of psychosis go on to develop a full-blown psychotic disorder. Thus, the inclusion of attenuated psychosis syndrome in Section III of *DSM-5* makes sense. Of those who seek help, it is estimated that 18% will meet the criteria for a psychotic disorder in the coming year; 32% will meet the criteria within 3 years; and others may develop depression or bipolar disorder with psychotic features, although the development of a schizophrenia spectrum disorder is more common.

Depressive Episodes With Short-Duration Hypomania

The proposed criteria for this condition for further study includes a lifetime experience of at least one major depressive episode with at least two hypomanic periods of at least 2 but less than 4 consecutive days. If the hypomanic symptoms last 4 days or more, the diagnosis would become bipolar II; if psychosis is present, it is by definition mania, and the diagnosis would be bipolar I. If the hypomanic features appear concurrently with a major depressive episode, the diagnosis would be major depressive disorder with mixed features. All of these disorders can be differentiated from cyclothymic disorder, because of the occurrence of at least one major depressive episode.

The prevalence rate of short-duration hypomania is unknown, but it may be more common in females who present with features of atypical depression. A family history of mania may be found, as well as a higher rate of suicide attempts than in healthy individuals. Substance use disorder, particularly alcohol use disorder, is commonly comorbid, as are anxiety disorders.

Persistent Complex Bereavement Disorder

Following the death of a loved one, a person may experience one or more of the following symptoms: yearning or longing for the deceased, intense sorrow, preoccupation with the deceased, or preoccupation with the circumstances surrounding his or her death. If the symptoms persist on most days for at least a 12-month period (6 months in the case of a child), and if the person experiences reactive distress to the death (e.g., disbelief, anger, avoidance) or social/identity disruption (e.g., expressed desire to die, isolation, confusion about life role, lack of interest in activities that once provided pleasure), then it would be considered persistent complex bereavement disorder. Specify if bereavement is a result of traumatic circumstances such as homicide or suicide.

Caffeine Use Disorder

Caffeine use is the only substance-related disorder that does not have a use disorder described in DSM-5, although caffeine tolerance and withdrawal are included. Caffeine use disorder, as included in Section III, is proposed for further study and includes a pattern of caffeine use and failure to control use despite negative consequences, such as heart, stomach, and urinary problems; symptoms of anxiety, depression, insomnia, and irritability; and difficulty concentrating (APA, 2013a). A distinction must be made between nonproblematic and problematic use of caffeine, given the high numbers of caffeine users in the general population.

Internet Gaming Disorder

This proposed disorder is based on more than 17 years of research, which indicates that Internet gaming has many of the basic hallmarks of an addiction (e.g., preoccupation with use, withdrawal symptoms, tolerance, loss of interest in other pursuits, unsuccessful attempts to quit, and usage to escape unpleasant feelings). People with Internet gaming disorder have been found to exhibit changes in the frontal lobe of the brain that controls attention, executive function, and emotion processing; some of the changes are comparable to the brains of people who are addicted to heroin and cocaine. Many recent studies point to the possibility of a genetic link in Internet addiction, as well as the possibility of changes in how the brain's dopamine system functions. Internet gaming disorder may be associated with major depressive disorder, ADHD, and OCD. In the case of online gambling, a diagnosis of gambling disorder must be ruled out.

Effective treatment for Internet gaming disorder would be similar to treatment for other addictions. Mindfulness-based strategies can help people recognize triggers to addictive behavior and find substitutes for the behavior. Cognitive behavior therapy can be effective in helping people change maladaptive cognitions that encourage pathological Internet usage (e.g., online sex, gambling). See *Selecting Effective Treatments* (Seligman & Reichenberg, 2012) for a complete discussion of evidence-based interventions for addictive disorders.

Neurobehavioral Disorder due to Prenatal Alcohol Exposure (ND-PAE)

Prenatal alcohol exposure has been shown to have a teratogenic effect on the central nervous system of the developing fetus. Proposed criteria for this disorder, which is estimated to affect 2% to 5% of the population prenatally, includes:

- Impaired neurocognitive functioning (e.g., IQ below 70, impaired executive functioning, impaired learning and memory)
- Impaired self-regulation (e.g., mood lability, frequent outbursts, impaired impulse control)
- Impairment in adaptive functioning (e.g., communication deficit, difficulty reading social cues, delayed ability to manage daily schedule)

Onset of ND-PAE must occur in childhood and must not be the result of postnatal use of substances. Research indicates that children with ND-PAE have more difficulties in school, poor employment records, legal trouble, and dependent living arrangements. Their risk of suicide is also higher, especially in late adolescence and early adulthood.

Nonsuicidal Self-Injury (NSSI)

Nonsuicidal self-injury is a maladaptive coping strategy that is frequently used to reduce emotional pain. NSSI is often, but not always, related to an increased risk of suicide. In *DSM-IV-TR*, self-injury was listed as a symptom of borderline personality disorder, which was the only category in which cutting or other self-harming behaviors appeared. Given a 12% to 23% prevalence rate of NSSI among nonclinical adolescent populations, clearly many teens who do not meet the criteria for borderline personality disorder are also in need of help, and some are at increased risk of accidental death from NSSI or as a result of later suicide attempts (Plener & Fegert, 2012; Washburn et al., 2012). Longitudinal studies have found a decline in rates of NSSI in adulthood, resulting in a larger focus on adolescents to help curb this very dangerous yet highly treatable condition.

Rates of NSSI appear to increase following media exposure and exposure to self-injurious practices shared on the Internet. Therefore, clinicians are advised to assess their adolescent clients' online behavior (Washburn et al., 2012). Although no treatment has been designed specifically for use with the high-risk adolescent population, current research is available about successful treatment for NSSI.

Therapeutic approaches to treating NSSI are similar to those used to treat self-harming behaviors in people with borderline personality disorder. Specifically, dialectical behavior therapy, schema-focused CBT, and mentalization-based treatment (MBT) modalities have been found to decrease suicidality and nonsuicidal self-harming behaviors. Physical activity and participation in organized sports have been found to be protective against NSSI behaviors in adolescence. Because of the alarming increase in the incidence of NSSI, research is currently underway to explore the effect of short-term problem-solving behavior and transdiagnostic treatment approaches. Seligman and Reichenberg (2012, pp. 374–377) provide a more in-depth discussion of treatment modalities for this important disorder, which can sometimes have lethal outcomes. Including NSSI in Section III of *DSM-5* sends a strong message that more research is needed.

Suicidal Behavior Disorder

Suicide is a leading cause of death worldwide. As many as 25% to 35% of persons who make one suicide attempt will make another. The risk of suicide increases with the co-occurrence of many of the mental disorders included in this book, including depression and bipolar disorders, disorders on the schizophrenia spectrum, anxiety and trauma-related disorders, eating disorders, and adjustment disorders. The inclusion of suicidal behavior disorder as a condition for further study in *DSM-5*, and the addition of suicide risk factors to appropriate disorders, are part of an ongoing recognition that despite efforts to reduce the number of people who take their own lives each year, the suicide rate has remained steady, at 10 to 13 suicides per 100,000 people, for more than 70 years. Tools for risk assessment and prevention may be found on the *DSM-5* website (www.DSM5.org) or in the Appendix of *Selecting Effective Treatments* (Seligman & Reichenberg, 2012).

Proposed criteria for suicidal behavior disorder include a suicide attempt within the last 24 months, which was self-initiated, was expected to lead to death, did not meet the criteria for nonsuicidal self-injury (which was described earlier), did not occur in a state of delirium or confusion, and was not undertaken solely for a political or religious objective. The diagnosis does not apply to suicidal ideation or preparatory acts in the absence of an attempt. Specify if "current" (not more than 12 months have elapsed since the last suicide attempt) or "in early remission" (12 to 24 months since the last attempt).

Suicidal behavior is difficult to predict. One study found that as many as 76% of people who completed suicide while inpatients in a psychiatric hospital had denied any suicidal ideation in the week preceding their deaths (Busch, Fawcett, & Jacobs, 2003). Other research confirms that neither psychiatrists nor the patients themselves were able to predict future suicide (Nock, Hwang, Sampson, & Kessler, 2010). Current research is underway to determine other methods of identifying people who are at high risk of suicide (Tingley, 2013). Readers are reminded that if clinically significant manifestations of these proposed disorders occur, they may be coded as Other Specified.

CONCLUSION
THE FUTURE OF DIAGNOSIS AND TREATMENT PLANNING

We come now to the end of *DSM-5 Essentials*. The text closes with a look at the future of diagnosis. We can expect continued research on the neurobiological underpinnings of disorders, increased requirements for evidence-based practice, new treatment delivery methods through apps, social media, and e-therapy, and the continued evolution of the two classification systems currently necessary to the diagnosis of mental disorders: the *DSM* and the *ICD*.

Treatment methodologies will also evolve. Transdiagnostic or cross-cutting symptom approaches that address similar symptoms across a variety of conditions continue to grow in popularity as a cost-effective way to target specific behaviors and provide symptom relief. Similarly, addressing anger and irritability as symptoms can help people with mood disorders, anxiety, conduct disorders, and some personality disorders learn to make more self-informed choices. Initial research indicates that adjunctive group therapy can be helpful in providing symptom relief across diagnoses.

I am happy to see the addition of cultural formularies, interviews, and a glossary to the fifth edition of the *DSM*. Future enhancements will no doubt accompany the completion of *ICD-11* in 2015 and keep pace with developments in science, research, and medicine. It is hoped that as new information and research becomes available, timely updates to the *Diagnostic and Statistical Manual* will allow practitioners to provide the most current diagnosis and treatments available. And in the future the *DSM-5* will be more closely linked to WHO's *ICD-11*, which is currently under development.

With all of the changes around us, one thing remains certain: Behavioral health care of the future will continue to focus on matching the best evidence-based treatments with the specific diagnosis to generate more treatment gains. Not only do third-party payors and managed care organizations want results, but clients, families, and therapists should be demanding them too! Matching the client's needs with the best evidence-based treatments is an important focus of research, and I believe it will continue to be, long into the future.

REFERENCES

Alexander, J., Goldschmidt, A. B., & LeGrange, D. (2013). *A clinician's guide to binge eating disorder*. New York, NY: Routledge.

American Psychiatric Association. (2013a). *Diagnostic and statistical manual of mental disorders* (5th ed.). Arlington, VA: Author.

American Psychiatric Association. (2013b). *Making a case for new disorders*. Retrieved from http://www.psychiatry.org/practice/dsm/dsm5

American Psychological Association. (2012). Transition to the ICD-10-CM: What does it mean for psychologists? *Practice Central*. Retrieved from http://www.apapracticecentral.org/update/2012/02-09/transition.aspx

Barbaresi, W. J., Colligan, R. C., Weaver, A. L., Voigt, R. G., Killian, J. M., & Katusic, S. K. (2013). Mortality, ADHD, and psychosocial adversity in adults with childhood ADHD: A prospective study. *Pediatrics, 131*, 637–644.

Busch, K. A., Fawcett, J., & Jacobs, D. G. (2003). Clinical correlates of inpatient suicide. *Journal of Clinical Psychiatry, 64*(1), 14–19.

Cunningham J., Yonkers, K. A., O'Brien, S., & Eriksson, E. (2009). Update on research and treatment of premenstrual dysphoric disorder. *Harvard Review of Psychiatry, 17*, 120–137.

DSM-5 Childhood and Adolescent Disorders Work Group. (2010). *Asperger's disorder proposed revisions: Disorders usually first diagnosed in infancy, childhood, or adolescence, DSM-5 development*. Arlington, VA: American Psychiatric Association. Retrieved from http://www.dsm5.org/ProposedRevisions/Pages/proposed revision.aspx?rid=97#

Epperson, C. N., Steiner, M., Hartlage, S. A., Eriksson, E., Schmidt, P. J., Jones, I., & Yonkers, K. A. (2012). Premenstrual dysphoric disorder: Evidence for a new category for *DSM-5*. *American Journal of Psychiatry*, 1–11. Retrieved from http://psychiatryonline.org/data/Journals/AJP/0/appi.ajp.2012.11081302.pdf

Frazier, T. W., Youngstrom, E. A., Speer, L., Embacher, R., Law, P., Constantino, J., . . . Eng, C. (2012). Validation of proposed *DSM-5* criteria for Autism Spectrum Disorder. *Journal of the American Association of Child and Adolescent Psychiatry, 51*, 28–40.

Friedman, R. A., & Leon, A. C. (2007). Expanding the black box—Depression, antidepressants, and the risk of suicide. *New England Journal of Medicine, 356*, 2343–2346.

Jones, K. D. (2012). Dimensional and cross-cutting assessments in the *DSM-5. Journal of Counseling and Development, 90,* 481–487.

Leibenluft, E. (2011). Severe mood dysregulation, irritability, and the diagnostic boundaries of bipolar disorder in youth. *American Journal of Psychiatry, 168,* 129–142.

Lembke, A. (2013, May 9). When it comes to addiction, the DSM-5 gets it right, but . . . *Pacific Standard.* Retrieved from http://www.psmag.com/health/when-it-comes-to-addiction-the-DSM-5-gets-it-right-but-57203

Lembke, A., Bradley, K. A., Henderson, P., Moos, R., & Harris, A. H. (2011). What the future holds. *Journal of General Internal Medicine, 26,* 777–782.

Mao, A. R., & Yen, J. (2010). Review of proposed changes in child and adolescent psychiatry diagnostic criteria for DSM-Version 5. *Child & Adolescent Psychopharmacology News, 15*(3), 1–8.

Montano, B. (2004). Diagnosis and treatment of ADHD in adults in primary care. *Journal of Clinical Psychiatry, 65*(Suppl 3), 18–21.

Nock, M. K., Hwang, I., Sampson, N. A., & Kessler, R. C. (2010). Mental disorders, comorbidity and suicidal behavior: Results from the National Co-morbidity Survey Replication. *Molecular Psychiatry, 15,* 868–876.

O'Brien, C. P. (2012, July). Rationale for changes in DSM-5. *Journal of Studies on Alcohol and Drugs, 73*(4), 705. Available at www.jsad.com/jsad/link/73/705

Pearlstein, T., & Steiner, M. (2008). Premenstrual dysphoric disorder: Burden of illness and treatment update. *Journal of Psychiatry and Neuroscience, 33,* 299–301.

Plener, P. L., & Fegert, J. J. (2012). Non-suicidal self-injury: State of the art perspective of a proposed new syndrome for DSM V [sic]. *Child and Adolescent Psychiatry and Mental Health, 6,* 9.

Seligman, L., & Reichenberg, L.W. (2012). *Selecting effective treatments: A comprehensive, systematic guide to treating mental disorders* (4th ed.). Hoboken, NJ: Wiley.

Seligman, L., & Reichenberg, L.W. (2013). *Theories of counseling and psychotherapy: Systems, strategies and skills* (4th ed.). New York, NY: Pearson.

Schuckit, M. A. (2012, July). Editor's corner: Editorial in reply to the comments of Griffith Edwards. *Journal of Studies on Alcohol and Drugs, 73*(4), 521–522. Available at www.jsad.com/jsad/link/73/521

Tingley, K. (2013, June 30). I'm not okay: Uncovering the self-destructive impulse that many people hide even from themselves. *New York Times Magazine,* pp. 23–27, 46–47.

Washburn, J. J., Richardt, S. L., Styer, D. M., Gebhardt, M., Juzwin, K. R., Yourek, A., & Aldridge, D. (2012). Psychotherapeutic approaches to non-suicidal self-injury in adolescents. *Child and Adolescent Psychiatry and Mental Health, 6.*

Washburn, J. J., West, A. E., & Heil, J. A. (2011). Treatment of pediatric bipolar disorder: A review. *Minerva Psichiatrica, 52,* 21–33.

World Health Organization. (2010). *International classification of diseases* (10th ed.). Retrieved from http://www.who.int/classifications/icd/en/

ABOUT THE AUTHOR

Lourie Wilson Reichenberg is a licensed professional counselor and the author of numerous books on counseling and psychology. Her most recent book, *Selecting Effective Treatments: A Comprehensive, Systematic Guide to Treating Mental Disorders*, 4th edition (Wiley, 2013), has recently been revised to incorporate a *DSM-5* update. She is currently at work on a companion piece entitled *Implementing Effective Treatments* (Wiley, forthcoming), which will help clinicians choose, understand, and match appropriate treatment strategies to diagnoses. She is also coauthor with Linda Seligman of *Theories of Counseling and Psychotherapy*, 3rd edition (Pearson, 2012).

Reichenberg received her bachelor's degree from Michigan State University and a master's degree in counseling psychology from Marymount University. She has taught graduate and undergraduate psychology and continues to provide education and training on the diagnosis and treatment of mental disorders, suicide assessment and prevention, and mindfulness. She provides supervision to counselors-in-residence and to interns at The Women's Center, in Vienna, Virginia. She works with individuals and couples in her private practice in Falls Church, Virginia, and is particularly interested in helping families that have been impacted by the presence of severe mental illness.

She has served on the boards of CrisisLink, the Virginia Association of Clinical Counselors, and Northern Virginia Licensed Professional Counselors (NVLPC), and is a member of the American Mental Health Counselors Association and the Association for the Development of the Person-Centered Approach, as developed by Carl Rogers.

Reichenberg has contributed her editing and writing skills to numerous publications, professional newsletters, trade magazines, and books: Her chapter on grief and loss was recently published in *Crisis Assessment, Intervention, and Prevention* (Pearson, 2013).

She lives in McLean, Virginia, with her husband of 25 years, Neil, surrounded by her books and papers; her grandchildren Izaak, Jaycee, and Orion; her son Al; and a Brittany Spaniel named Bogey.

AUTHOR INDEX

SUBJECT INDEX